Issues Facing Society

Titles in the School of the Word series:

A Life of Worship	John Johnson & Mike Stevens
According to Your Faith	Bryn Jones
Battle for the Mind	Stephen Matthew
Be Eager to Prophesy	Hugh Thompson
Called to be a Disciple	Dale Barnes
Christian Manhood	David Matthew
Effective Prayer	Bryn Jones
Essential Foundations	Hugh Thompson
Excelling as a Woman	Barbie Reynolds
Fulfilment in Marriage	Hugh & Rosemary Thompson
Go and Make Disciples	Hugh Thompson
Issues Facing Society	John Houghton
Living in the Anointing	Paul Scanlon
Money Matters	Stephen Matthew
More Than Conquerors	Don Silber
Realities of the New Creation	Dale Barnes
Secure in God	Tony & Margaret Howson
Successful Parents	Hugh & Rosemary Thompson
Woman: Created for Success	Barbie Reynolds
Woman: Living in Victory	Barbie Reynolds

Issues Facing Society

John Houghton

Harvestime

Published in the United Kingdom by:
Harvestime Publishing Ltd, 69 Main Street
Markfield, Leicester LE6 0UT

First published by Harvestime
First printed June 1988
Reprinted with additional material
January 1992

ISBN 0-947714-52-9

Typeset in the United Kingdom by:
ScribeTech Ltd, Bradford BD8 7BX

Printed and bound in Great Britain by:
BPCC Hazell Books, Aylesbury
Bucks, England
Member of BPCC Ltd

Increasing numbers of people are wanting to study the Word of God in depth. To go to a Bible college or seminary is not feasible for the majority, yet they desire more than the average church is able to provide in its teaching curriculum.

The book you are about to study is part of a library of components that together provide a comprehensive overview of the Scriptures in relation to life. Each book is complete in itself but is developed in such a way that the best result is experienced by studying it as part of the whole series.

We have produced the curriculum so that each component, in addition to its use as a personal study, can provide a teaching programme for study in church, home, college campus, school, military base, prison or any other group setting.

It is our prayer that you will be greatly enriched in your spiritual development through this book.

Bryn Jones
Founder — School of the Word

Getting the Most Out of This Study

This School of the Word study book is one of a series designed to relate Bible truths to everyday life. Each of the lessons starts with a direct search of the Scriptures and ends with a challenge to the student to apply the truths discovered. As the blank spaces left in Bible verses are filled in, the most important words and phrases stand out clearly on the page.

The material can be used in a number of different ways. It can form the basis of an individual study or be used in a group setting over a number of weeks. But experience has shown that it has the greatest benefit when a group of people study it together under a leader who is well prepared.

Tips for Leaders

If you are a leader planning to take a number of people through this study, you should consider the following:

1. Be prepared

It is essential that you do the whole study in advance yourself. This will help you to be conversant with the basic outline and have a feeling for the level of teaching based on it that your students can take.

2. Keep to the outline

It is important to keep to the outline contained in this study. This has been carefully designed to build principle on principle, 'precept upon precept' (Isaiah 28:10 RAV), with the eventual aim of the student becoming 'thoroughly equipped for every good work' (2 Timothy 3:17).

Whatever happens, don't allow your teaching to digress and become an opportunity to preach an hour's sermon!

3. Use your own experience

Even though you are staying with the outline, where possible introduce additional illustrations and applications drawn from your own experience. This makes the basic teaching more relevant to the local setting. In addition, you may wish to add more emphasis to certain points.

4. Avoid indigestion

Each lesson should take about an hour to complete. You may like to divide this into two half-hour sessions by arranging a short break for coffee and a chat halfway through. That way, the teaching is kept to manageable portions.

In some cases you may feel that the group discussion is of such vital importance to your local area that you want to spread each lesson over two weeks. If you do this, try to divide the questions at the end so that they are relevant to that week's teaching.

5. Have the right tools

Make sure that all the students have access to a copy of the New International Version of the Bible — upon which the book is based. Encourage them to fill in the blank spaces in advance but to leave answering the true/false questions until after each teaching session.

Tips for Students

Before you start the study you need to ask yourself: Am I really committed to growing as a disciple of Jesus Christ? If the answer is yes, then you're ready to proceed. Here are some immediate steps you can take to ensure maximum benefit from the course:

1. Determine your goal

This book is designed to help you achieve God's goal and destiny for you. It doesn't matter whether you are young or old, a recent convert or someone who has been a Christian for many years.

Today you are taking a step towards the fulfilment of your destiny.

Look ahead and see yourself as God desires you to be. Then confess your commitment: 'This is the kind of person I *will* become.'

2. Plan your progress

Your faith commitment to work through this book, and so take one more step towards becoming the person God intends you to be, must not only be pursued but measured in its progress. The apostle Paul said:

> *'By the grace given me I say to every one of you: Do not think of yourself more highly than you ought, but rather think of yourself with sober judgment, in accordance with the measure of faith God has given you.'*
>
> (Romans 12:3)

You know the kind of person you already are. You know the level of commitment you already have in your life. Now from this point determine how much time per day or week you are prepared to give to the study of the Word of God to achieve your goal.

At the end of each lesson in this study-book there is an opportunity for you to complete assignments and answer some Bible-based questions. This helps to fix the Word of God more firmly in your heart, and thus provide a reservoir of truth that the Holy Spirit can draw upon in the training of your life.

3. Recruit to the study course

Fellowship is one of the keys to Christian growth. The word 'fellowship' comes from the Greek word *koinonia*, which means to 'share things in common'.

Nothing will facilitate your progress as much as encouraging others to share in the same study programme with you, either on a personal basis or in a group. Share with each other the things you are learning and discovering in the Word of God and in life.

In this way you will be able to practise together much of what you study, and so strengthen each other in faith, just as 'iron sharpens iron' (Proverbs 27:17).

4. Set and maintain your standards

If this study is to be of maximum benefit to you, it must not be hurried. It is no use merely reading the written material and rushing the assignment. The book is designed to provoke you to your own searching and thinking, and to a demonstration of faith in God.

5. Check your progress

Once you have worked right through the book, ask your pastor or church leader to read through your answers. If he is satisfied that you have done your best to complete the questions, get him to send us a note to this effect. We will then forward a certificate for him to sign and present to you.

Your pastor is also the best person to monitor your progress and share your zeal to develop as a Christian disciple. If you are at college, university or in the armed forces, or for some other reason have no immediate access to a pastor, send us your book enclosing return postage and we will send it back to you with your certificate.

School of the Word
Harvestime Publishing Ltd
69 Main Street
Markfield
Leicester LE6 0UT
UK

Contents

Unless otherwise stated, Scripture quotations are taken from the New International Version.

Other versions referred to in this series include the New American Standard Bible (NASB), the Revised Authorised Version (RAV) and the Amplified Bible (Amp).

Verses have blank spaces for you to insert the missing words as you follow the Scriptures. This will deepen the impact of the Bible in your life.

Introduction

Should the church take any interest in the great moral questions which confront society? Or should church leaders see their role merely as supplying a 'religious' dimension to life – conducting baptisms, weddings and funerals, providing church services and marking the passing of the seasons with appropriate festivals?

'Let the scientists, sociologists and politicians deal with the real world,' some would say.

Or again, is the role of the church simply to preach the gospel in the power of the Spirit? If men and women repent and believe in sufficient numbers and with enough miracles taking place, then all society's problems will be solved. Or will they?

The Old Testament prophets continually preached against religion which had no concern for the daily plight of men and women. Isaiah cries, 'Is not this the kind of fasting I have chosen: to loose the chains of injustice and untie the cords of the yoke, to set the oppressed free . . . to share your food with the hungry . . . to provide the poor wanderer with shelter . . . to clothe him?' (Isaiah 58:6-7).

Jesus addressed all the great issues of his day in the course of his gospel ministry. Kingdom power would be revealed in Good Samaritans, in prison visitors, in those who gave to the poor, in new marriage ethics, political attitudes and protection of the weak.

All the New Testament letters reflect the Master's concern that the good news should touch every aspect of life. Indeed, Paul sees a day coming when God will reconcile all things through his Son.

The cross is the great road-junction of life, the meeting-place of heaven and hell, life and death, justice and injustice, the rich and the poor, men and women, religion and politics. Obey the signals and we drive up Reconciliation Road; disobey them and we crash.

Preaching the gospel of the kingdom involves bringing the government of God into every department of life. Concern for society, its values and practices, is a central part of the church's mission. We are called to bring God's reconciliation to God's world.

This study course is about just that. In the eight lessons we will consider the main issues of our day, the biblical principles which apply to them and some of the practical things we can do about them.

By its very nature, this is only an introduction to a vast field, but my hope is that it will both stimulate our concern and set us thinking along the right lines.

Peace

Jeremiah's accusation, ' "Peace, peace," they say, when there is no peace' (Jeremiah 6:14) was never more aptly fulfilled than in 1938 when British Prime Minister, Neville Chamberlain, declared, 'Peace in our time'. World War Two broke out in September 1939.

We live in a world of unceasing war. Our greatest investments of wealth, ingenuity and energy are concentrated, not on the relief of sickness and famine, but on a programme of 'how to kill your neighbour more effectively than he can kill you'!

The sheer cost of all this is staggering. International arms deals total £16 billion a year. An estimated twenty million people have died in wars since World War Two – nearly all of them in Third World countries. The recent Gulf War took the lives of an estimated two hundred and fifty thousand Iraqis.

In our madness we have developed the capacity for total self-annihilation. The grim spectre of the nuclear mushroom-cloud haunts us all.

Much as we welcome the easing of East-West tensions and the consequent reductions in strategic missiles, the USA and Russia still have between them enough nuclear warheads to destroy the world several times over. Soviet leader Mikhail Gorbachev has said, 'Today, just one strategic submarine carries a destructive potential equal to several Second World Wars, and there are dozens of such submarines.'

To this we must add the growing threat posed by the development of nuclear weapons in unstable Third World nations, whose leaders may have less qualms about their deployment than their Western counterparts.

We are living dangerously close to the brink.

With the escalation of conventional wars, the rise of international terrorism and the increase in crimes of violence on our streets, we have a situation where people's hearts fail them for fear.

Is there any word from the Lord concerning this, the second horseman of the Apocalypse? We believe there is.

1. The Root Cause of War

a. The Fall

War and violence is a direct result of the Fall. The poisonous root of Adam and Eve's disobedience soon began to produce bitter fruit in their offspring:

> *'Cain said to his brother Abel, "Let's go out to the field." And while they were in the field, Cain ______________ his brother Abel and ____________ ______.'*
>
> (Genesis 4:8)

b. A heart issue

Violence is endemic in the hearts of men and women. Jesus said, 'Out of the heart come evil thoughts, murder . . .' (Matthew 15:19).

> *'What causes __________ and ______________ among you? Don't they come from your ____________ that battle within you? You ________ something but don't get it. You ______ and __________, but you cannot have what you want. You ____________ and __________.'*
>
> (James 4:1-2)

c. Greed

Covetousness (or greed) is the major sin that initiates war.

Cain wanted Abel's blessing. John the Baptist was executed because Herod wanted to continue in an unlawful marriage. Nations go to war because they become greedy for power, or land, or natural resources – or even religious domination. Read what follows from the above passage:

'You do not have, because you do not ask God. When you ask, you do not receive, because you ask with wrong motives, that you may spend what you get on your pleasures.'

(James 4:2-3)

'Everything in the world – the ______________ of sinful man, the ________ of his eyes and the ________________ of what he has and does – comes not from the Father but from the world.'

(1 John 2:16)

Greed devours its victims. Countless peoples have been driven reluctantly to defend their homes, their loved ones and their lands because of the rapacity of others. Who can compute the grief of the millions bereaved in the battle for liberty? A weeping world cries out for *peace*.

Only the gospel brings true and lasting peace because it alone tackles the root issues and brings us under the reign of the Prince of Peace. This should make the church of Jesus Christ the greatest peace movement in the world.

Sadly, such has not always been the case. Alliances with the state have generally meant a compromise with the world. Too often the cross has preceded the sword and the name of Jesus been invoked to justify mass slaughter.

Much support for state-religious aggression has been drawn from the Old Testament. We need to consider this.

2. The Old Testament Approach to War

Many see a stark contrast between the Old and New Testaments on the subject of war and violence. Indeed, some have gone so far as to suggest that we are dealing with two different Gods! This is hardly the case, so we must look a little closer at what the Old Testament does have to say.

a. Violence grieves the heart of God

'The Lord was grieved that he had made man on the earth, and his heart was filled with pain.'

(Genesis 6:6)

Why was this so? Read Genesis 6:11-13. What was the earth filled with? There is no suggestion here of a war-mongering God delighting in violence.

What we do encounter in the Old Testament, however, is a holy God who is the righteous Judge of all the earth.

b. Wars of judgment

The Canaanites were particularly vile sinners – not only were they sexually very immoral but they also sacrificed live children to the god Molech. Such sins, if allowed to continue unabated, would sooner or later have polluted the whole world.

God's people were called to be pure so that they could be the channel for re-establishing God's righteousness in the earth. They were also commanded to perform a clean-up operation on his behalf. Read Leviticus 18:24-25. What was not to be defiled? What would happen if God's people defiled it?

Read Deuteronomy 7:1-6. Note particularly verse 5 and jot down the things the people were to do. Notice that these actions were all inspired by their faith. God's people were not to be motivated by covetousness for land but by jealousy for the name of the Lord.

c. A free choice

Fighting was never compulsory for the Israelites. They were not to be a war-like nation. What are the four reasons given for a man to be excused fighting (Deuteronomy 20:5-9)?

d. Trust in the Lord

God's people were instructed to look to him for their defence. In particular they were not to trust in the ultimate weapon of their day, which was the horse-drawn chariot. This travelled at a phenomenal twenty miles per hour – a speed, incidentally, which was not exceeded by any road vehicle until 1880!

Joshua 11:4-9 records God's anti-escalation of armaments policy – captured chariots are to be destroyed:

> *'You are to hamstring their horses and burn their chariots.'*
>
> (Joshua 11:6)

The notion of spiritual protection is clear in the Old Testament. What, according to Isaiah 31:1, is pronounced upon those who trust in their own weapons rather than the Lord?

Read the story of Elisha and his servant in 2 Kings 6:8-23. What did Elisha pray for his servant? What did the servant see?

God's supernatural protection extended also to the city of Jerusalem. The Assyrian army, having conquered everything else in its path, reached the walls of Jerusalem in 701 BC. Isaiah 37:14-20, 33-37 records the astonishing events. What lessons can we learn from this?

Zechariah 9:9-10 gives us a tremendous promise associated with the coming of the Messiah. What is it?

To summarise, the Old Testament nowhere advances a power philosophy to justify imperialist expansion. When violence is advocated, it is always for the purification of God's earth. His people were not to seek advantage in sophisticated weaponry but were rather to trust their cause to him.

3. The New Testament Approach to Violence

a. A violent age

Jesus recognised and prophesied that this age would be characterised by war:

> *'You will hear of ________ and ________________________________,*
> *but see to it that you are not alarmed. Such things must happen,*
> *but the end is still to come. ____________ will rise ____________*
> *__________, and kingdom against kingdom.'*
>
> (Matthew 24:6-7)

The book of Revelation speaks continually of the strife of sinful men but also of God using war as an instrument of his righteous judgment. Revelation 9 is a good example of this and reminds us of the continuity between the revelation of the Old Testament and that of the New.

In a vivid picture of a Lamb opening a seven-sealed scroll (Revelation 6:1 – 8:5), we are taught that Jesus is in ultimate control of world history. This is no 'gentle Jesus meek and mild' – read Revelation 19:11-16 – but the awesome Lord of glory who rules with a rod of iron.

b. Love your enemies

Against this backdrop to world history, Jesus both taught and practised non-violence:

> *'Blessed are the ________________________, for they will be called sons of God.'*
>
> (Matthew 5:9)

Read Matthew 5:38-48 for an astonishing new ethic that applied not only to civil enemies but also to the occupying Roman army. Love in this context doesn't mean personal endearment – they were, after all, enemies – but it does mean consideration and kindness. Paul has the same thought in Romans 12:17-21. We are called to be a law-abiding people of peace.

There is no way that the kingdom of God is to be extended by physical violence – John 6:15; 18:33-38. This rules out the idea of crusades or holy wars.

4. The Gospel of Peace

a. The Prince of Peace

The birth of Jesus was announced in terms of peace – Luke 2:14. Isaiah prophesied that wars would end wherever he reigned. Note in particular the last of the four titles given to Jesus in Isaiah 9:6.

b. Peace through the cross

> *'He himself is our __________, who has made the two one and has ____________________ the barrier, the dividing wall of ____________________ . . . . His purpose was to create in himself one new man out of the two, thus making __________, and in this one body to __________________ both of them to God through the __________, by which he put to death their hostility. He came and preached peace to you who were far away and peace to those who were near.'*
>
> (Ephesians 2:14-17)

c. New people, new society

The gospel transforms both our inner nature and our outer conduct. It removes the covetousness and the anger from our souls.

> *'We lived in _____________ and _________, being __________ and _____________ one another. But when the ________________ and _________ of God our Saviour appeared, he _________ us.'*
>
> (Titus 3:3-5)

The more this gospel spreads, the greater the prospects for peace in our time, in the streets, in the nation, in the world.

5. What are God's People to Do?

We have a positive contribution to make in mitigating the worst effects of sin. As light we show the way; as salt we slow down the putrefaction. Although we cannot absolutely prevent war we can make a marked difference.

a. We are to pray

War is more likely to occur when our prayers fail.

Look up 1 Timothy 2:1-4. Why is this prayer such a priority (v3-4)? As we pray, we are to recognise the sovereignty of God over the affairs of this world. Jesus is King of kings and Lord of lords.

We must also recognise a satanic strategy. In spite of stories of servicemen coming to the Lord, war hinders the gospel – and nuclear war hinders the gospel absolutely. The devil would love to pre-empt Christ's return for his bride by engineering a nuclear holocaust which would destroy the human race. Our prayers can prevent it.

b. Live in hope

Read Psalm 91 and write in your own words what it promises. We are to put faith in God, not in people. We must refuse the fear of this generation. Our concern about nuclear war must not be first to save our own skins but to see God's purposes achieved. Instead of cowering we are to conquer.

c. Fight the good fight

We are called to spiritual warfare. This is our holy war:

> '*We do not wage war as the world does. The weapons we fight with are not the weapons of the world. On the contrary, they have* _______________ _____________ *to* ___________________ ______________________. *We demolish arguments and every pretension that sets itself up against the knowledge of God.*'
>
> (2 Corinthians 10:3-5)

Read Ephesians 6:10-20. Who is the enemy (v12)? Consider each piece of armour, noting that some are for defence, some for attack.

d. Do good to all people

If we find ourselves in a conflict situation, our first concern must be to alleviate suffering. This may be by doing medical work or by sacrificing our lives to save others.

This latter is the dilemma for peace-loving Christians. Do we defend our loved ones – even if we may have to kill or be killed in the process? Doesn't fighting sometimes minimise suffering in the long run? Isn't it good to break tyranny even if that involves the use of force? We want to be pacifists but circumstances can appear on occasions to make that untenable.

We must obey our conscience. Whether we fight in these circumstances or declare ourselves to be conscientious objectors, it will take courage to serve the good of others. What we must not do is to glorify war or take delight in revenge. Blood-lust has no place in the hearts of those cleansed by the blood of Christ.

e. Preach righteousness

We must speak out against unrighteousness, not only as it is found in individuals, but where it is institutional and political. As peacemakers we must advocate reductions in international tension – that includes a realistic multilateral disarmament policy, both of nuclear and conventional weapons.

Righteousness exalts a nation – even Sodom and Gomorrah could have been spared if sufficient righteous people had been found (Genesis 18:20-33). Proclaiming the gospel will turn many to righteousness and bring peace in our land.

This is our distinctive contribution to society and we must become confident enough to share it. 'Righteousness marches' will achieve more for peace than 'peace marches'!

****

LESSON 1

Peace

True or False

1. T F Greed is the major sin that initiates war.
2. T F God's attitude to war in the Old Testament is different from that in the New Testament.
3. T F God never uses violence to judge anyone.
4. T F Jesus refused to use earthly weapons and techniques to establish his kingdom.

5. T F Jesus taught us to love those who hate us.

6. T F Criticism, anger and malice are all right in the church provided we don't actually get physical about it.

7. T F God's people have no reason to fear the future.

8. T F As people of peace we need to speak out against unrighteousness in society.

Group Discussion

1. Read the following and discuss the questions raised:

During the first two centuries of church history God's people held to a non-violent stance. This may be summarised in Tertullian's statement that 'Christ, in disarming Peter, ungirt every soldier'.

The pagan philosopher, Cicero, wanting to control the awful excesses of warfare, came up with the theory of 'just war' (as distinct from unjust war). When the church became allied with the state, under Augustine's influence it adopted this as the Christian position. This has largely been the position in the Western world ever since.

Briefly, the just war theory states that: only defensive war is legitimate; the intention must be to obtain peace; it must be the last resort; there must be a formal declaration; it must be fought with limited objectives and weaponry; non-participants must be immune from attack.

The just war theory has failed because of its initial commitment to violence. It has a history of 'brakes failure'.

Nuclear weapons in any case render the just war theory null and void. Most Christians are agreed that the use of nuclear weapons is immoral. But should they be retained as a deterrent?

Jesus instructed us to turn the other cheek. Does this mean that a Christian should refuse to defend himself when being assaulted in the street or should stand passively by while a friend or relative is being assaulted?

Granted that a nation should not attack another nation for unworthy motives, is it right to seek to liberate another nation from tyranny? Is it right for a nation operating on Christian principles to defend itself against tyranny?

Personal Assignment

1. Pray for international peace every day for a week and then build this into your prayer life on a regular basis.

2. Read the book of Revelation right through at one sitting to get an overall picture. Don't worry about trying to understand every detail (for further help see *Revelation – Meaningful mysteries for today*, by Terry Brooks, Harvestime).

3. Deliberately check in your heart that you have forgiven everyone you can remember who has harmed you.

True or False

1.T 2.F 3.F 4.T 5.T 6.F 7.T 8.T

Human Rights

The United Nations declaration of human rights proclaims the right:

- ☐ to life, to freedom from subjection to torture, inhuman or degrading treatment or punishment, or to slavery, servitude or forced labour
- ☐ to liberty and security of the person
- ☐ to a fair trial
- ☐ to freedom from retroactive criminal laws or punishments
- ☐ to respect for private and family life, home and correspondence
- ☐ to freedom of thought, conscience and religion
- ☐ to freedom of expression, peaceful expression and association
- ☐ to an effective remedy against officials who violate these rights
- ☐ to the enjoyment of these rights without discrimination on any ground such as sex, race, colour, language, religion, political or other opinion, national or social origin, association with a national minority, property, birth or other status

Today, the majority of the people in the world are held in a bondage which denies all or most of the UN declaration. And even where democracy holds sway, human rights are seriously limited for many groups. Justice still works best for Western, white, wealthy males!

The declaration is an example of idealism. It is an aspiration to human freedom in a world of political, racial, economic, sexual and religious bondage.

1. Christianity and Human Rights

Christians are not idealists, but neither are they indifferent to human bondage and deprivation. Jesus' message of freedom is the greatest single contribution to human rights in history. Here is his Nazareth Manifesto:

> *'To preach good news to the poor . . . . To proclaim freedom for the prisoners and recovery of sight for the blind, to release the oppressed, to proclaim the year of the Lord's favour'.*
>
> (Luke 4:18-19)

This has enormous spiritual implications largely ignored by modern society, but it also declares Jesus' concern for the liberation of the whole person.

Yet Christians have sometimes become the persecutors. Christianity – the state version – has a bad record on human rights. Slavery, torture, class barriers, sexual subjugation, colonialism and many more vices have been justified in the name of the one who came to abolish injustice. The church has sinned grievously, and many of today's secular responses to human rights reflect a recognition of that fact.

In particular, communism would never have emerged as a world force if the church had been the prophetic and reforming agent on behalf of the oppressed.

Marxism, and its christianised form known as liberation theology, stands in stark contrast to the authentic New Testament church – violent confrontation versus healing love and persuasive wisdom. Yet if liberation theology is a Christian extreme, then so is an evangelicalism concerned only with salvation from personal sin and with preserving the faithful until they go to heaven. Jesus' message implies far more than this.

2. A Biblical Approach to Human Rights

The issue of human rights confronts us squarely with the question, 'What is man?'

a. A marred image

The gospel begins with creation. Man is dust into which God has breathed. Not too high, certainly not too low – he is midway between the angels and the animals (Psalm 8:3-8).

Man (or humankind) was created in two forms – male and female. Both were in the image of God, both were to have authority, both were made without reference to racial, social or intellectual characteristics. Alienation, between themselves and God, and between one another, was unknown.

Yet today we are magnificent ruins, made in the image of God yet marred in every part. Our dignity was sacrificed through the Fall and the familiar story of human injustice soon appears. Romans 1:18-32 makes it clear that because man has wilfully and cleverly suppressed the truth about God and become idolatrous, God has given him over to depraved thinking. This expresses itself in evil, unjust living which among other things denies human rights (v18, 28-32).

b. A new heart

The gospel proposes a remedy. It isn't a political solution imposed upon unwilling people but a new heart, which in turn is reflected in a new society.

Read Hebrews 8:10-12. No longer is the law of God an outward ordinance to be reluctantly obeyed under threat of death. Instead it becomes a delight. This was prophetically written concerning Jesus:

> *'I desire to do ________ ______, O my God; your law is within ____ __________.'*
>
> (Psalm 40:8)

This means that the law is encapsulated in the new commandment to love one another (John 13:34-35). Romans 13:8-10 explains that love is not against law but is the proper way to fulfil God's good law.

c. A new status

If the new heart produces a new attitude of love towards our fellow-creatures, then the gospel of grace also changes our status. The old categories of race, class and sex lose their importance (Galatians 3:28-29). Instead,

> *'You are all ________ of ______ through faith in Christ Jesus.'*
>
> (Galatians 3:26)

God doesn't create this new equality by removing our distinctive characteristics. Instead he raises us all up to the status of the noblest of all, the Son of God.

Furthermore, he declares us all to be members of a chosen race, not based on earthly lineage, but on faith. As all human beings may put their faith in Christ, nobody is excluded on the grounds of natural birth or status. The gospel resolves absolutely the question of our personal identity.

All this was accomplished through the cross of Christ and has immediate implications for the way in which we live together. But before we come to this, we must consider some political implications of belonging to a new society.

d. A political solution?

Grace must affect politics but politics cannot produce grace. This is why Jesus would not lead a political revolution. He refused the position when offered:

> *'Jesus, knowing that they intended to come and make him __________ by ____________, __________________ again to a mountain by himself.'*
>
> (John 6:15)

For the same reason, he avoided an overt attack upon the repressive Roman government which, in his own nation, abused every known human right.

Jesus recognised the uncomfortable truth that the most dangerous thing you can give to a man is his freedom – unless grace operates to sanctify his conscience and to discipline his heart. All rights carry responsibility (Galatians 5:13).

This has always been the dilemma for state churches. They preach a message of moral responsibility but generally fail to proclaim converting grace. As a result, people don't behave. Depending upon their grasp of political power, such churches then become either ineffective or repressive – the Impotent or the Inquisition! Only grace guarantees human freedom.

Liberation theology, born out of frustration with a middle-class, pietistic church which gives to charity but ignores institutional evil, has for all its concern abandoned hope in grace. It has no place for supernatural intervention. In the end all we can do is resort to violence.

But we cannot embrace the ways of violence in order to achieve the goals of the Prince of Peace. Proclaiming the gospel of grace is the only sure remedy for injustice.

e. The right to rights

Human rights are not an absolute. Doing the will of God is. Christians are called to sacrifice their human rights for the sake of the gospel (Matthew 5:10-12, 38-42; 1 Peter 4:12-16). The Christian church is today probably the most heavily persecuted minority in the world. Religious liberty is purchased with martyrs' blood. This means, incidentally, that the believer can hardly be a supporter of religious persecution.

In this we follow the Master who at the cross willingly put himself into the hands of unjust men. The trial and crucifixion of Christ stand as one of the greatest denials of human rights in history. But it was the will of God (Isaiah 53:10)!

One of the ways we come into conflict with the powers that be is by speaking up for the needy. It is part of our calling:

> *'Speak up for those who cannot speak for themselves, for the rights of all who are destitute. _______________ and _____________ ; __________ the rights of the poor and needy.'*
>
> (Proverbs 31:8-9)

It is appropriate then to ask what our relationship with the state should be.

f. Duty to the state

What does the Christian owe to the state? Is it always right to obey its laws and dictates? When does duty to God come first? Should a Christian involve himself in revolutionary or socially disruptive action? Here are some pointers:

1. Government springs from the nature of God

Because government springs from God's nature, anarchy is as unacceptable now as it was in the days of the judges (Judges 21:25). The principle of government is given for the benefit of humankind (Romans 13:1-7; 1 Peter 2:13-14). List the benefits government brings.

The Scriptures don't recommend any particular type of secular government, but they have a lot to say about the responsibilities and accountability of national leaders. This remains true whether they are dictators or democratically elected. Democracy itself has no particular biblical support. Righteous government of any kind most certainly does.

2. God governs the nations

In spite of all the troubles, God is not far removed but intimately involved with his world. He organises the balance of power (Job 12:23-24) with a purpose:

> *'So that men would_________ _______ and perhaps reach out for him and _________ _______ .'*
>
> (Acts 17:27)

3. We do not belong to the world system (Colossians 1:13; Philippians 3:20)

Instead of being a part of the world system we are committed to a spiritual revolution (Acts 17:6-7). This sets limits upon what we can give to the state (Mark 12:17). We cannot give it what rightfully belongs to God. Our duty to him is higher and, if the state makes demands upon us contrary to the clear will of God, we must disobey it (Acts 5:29).

This may involve persecution, but let it be for the right reasons (1 Peter 3:17; 4:14-16). Nationalism must not become our god. However, Paul did have a 'sit-in' to get his Roman rights (Acts 16:37)! There is a place for non-violent protest.

4. We owe certain things to the state

We owe to the state:

- ☐ respect (Romans 13:7; 1 Peter 2:17)
- ☐ obedience (Romans 13:1; Titus 3:1; 1 Peter 2:13-14)
- ☐ taxes (Mark 12:13-17; Romans 13:6-7)
- ☐ prayer (1 Timothy 2:1-5)
- ☐ witness to Christ and the enlightening of public opinion with Christian values (Matthew 5:13-16)

We are at liberty to exercise democratic lobbying rights where we have them and to gain influence in high places by individual political involvement. (Because politics is the art of the possible, it is inappropriate to create a 'Christian' party, or for churches to commit themselves politically. We are to support all evidence of true righteousness, wherever we find it in the political spectrum.) We are also free to influence public opinion by publishing our views.

Our own community lifestyle should testify to the liberating power of the gospel. And that brings us to consider three specific areas where this should be so.

3. Race, Sex and Class

a. Jews and Gentiles

Read Ephesians 2:11-19. No greater divide existed in the ancient world than that between Jew and Gentile. It is difficult to imagine just how great was the impact when suddenly they began to live together in harmony. This is what the cross accomplished. Racial alienation is abolished when we become members of a new nation which embraces faith in Jesus.

Notice that the Council of Jerusalem did not require Gentile converts to embrace Jewish circumcision and ceremonial laws in order to become part of the Christian church (Acts 15:5-11, 28-29). Nor were Gentiles to be insensitive to Jewish scruples about food (Romans 14:1-6, 13-17).

The early church also dealt with tribal favouritism. Read Acts 6:1-7. What was the complaint? And how did they deal with it?

As Christians we are opposed to all forms of racism, including racial prejudice, discrimination, apartheid, whether blacks against whites or whites against blacks, because of our belief in the dignity of man. But we believe that only the gospel of grace can make this a reality.

We aren't opposed to racial *distinctiveness,* however. That is a part of human identity. As we embrace biblical principles together, so a new transcultural culture emerges which enables us to live in harmony and yet be enriched by our diversity.

b. Men and women

The battle of the sexes has its origin in the Fall. In Eden was born male chauvinism, female vulnerability and mutual mistrust. So evolved a society where Aristotle considered females to be imperfect males, accidentally produced by the father's inadequacy or by the malign influence of a moist south wind! And Josephus stated, 'The woman is inferior to the man in every way.'

The gospel restores the creational archetype – 'as it was in the beginning'. Eve was of co-equal status with Adam. Her role was as complementary helper to him in his leadership (Genesis 1:26-27). She was received as a gift from God and in no way inferior to Adam. They functioned as a unity. In the words of Peter Lombard (1157), 'Eve was not taken from the feet of Adam to be his slave, nor from his head to be his lord, but from his side to be his partner.'

Women are of equal status to men as regards salvation. In Christ –

> *'There is neither Jew nor Greek, slave nor free, ________ nor ____________, for you are ______ ______ in Christ Jesus.'*
>
> (Galatians 3:28)

But equal status doesn't imply sameness or loss of masculinity and femininity. The modern world confuses status with function and many feminists suggest that the traditional functions of homemaking or exercising feminine virtues imply lower status.

This can be true, but it doesn't have to be. Read Proverbs 31:10-31. Here was a woman with a home-based ministry that provided full scope for all her many talents.

There is nothing in Scripture to suggest that a creational archetype means a cultural stereotype. Women have the right to pursue a career and earn their own living. Married women don't have to do all the shopping, cooking, cleaning and baby-rearing. But neither should the latter calling be despised as unfulfilling or demeaning.

However, the creational archetype does throughout Scripture assign *a headship role to men.* That means they have the responsibility to lead, especially in marriage. Paul appeals to the priority of creation (1 Timothy 2:13), the mode of creation (1 Corinthians 11:8) and the purpose of creation (1 Corinthians 11:9) to uphold this.

Properly exercised male headship releases a woman to fulfil her calling and enjoy her God-given rights. It doesn't mean that any young man can, by virtue of his maleness, order women to submit to him! Read 1 Timothy 5:1-2 for the correct relational attitude.

(Note: The issue of women's ministry is confused by talking about rights because Christian ministry is not a right!)

(Note: It is perfectly appropriate that women should be afforded equal opportunities, pay and conditions with men, and be entitled to equal legal status and franchise.)

c. Slavery

The realism of the gospel meant that Christians were not encouraged to fight directly against slavery. At that time it would have been a futile exercise. Freedom was desirable (1 Corinthians 7:20-22) but was not the prime issue. Christian slaves were the Lord's freemen and should serve him in their situation (Ephesians 6:5-8).

However, the seeds for emancipation were sown by the early church. Masters are instructed to care for their slaves (Ephesians 6:9). Instead of treating them as animals they were to be considered the Lord's people.

Nowhere is this more clear than in the letter to Philemon. A recaptured runaway slave would normally be executed. Paul instructs Philemon to receive him back as a brother and to treat him as though he were the apostle himself (Philemon 15-17). The implications of this are very far-reaching. The axe was laid to the root of slavery. What a tragedy it took so long for the wretched tree to be felled!

Nor is it entirely dead. Slavery still exists in many parts of the world. That is to say nothing of economic slavery which binds multitudes in subhuman conditions, usually for the material benefit of the affluent West. We should not remain silent about this.

****

LESSON 2

Human Rights

True or False

1. T F Christianity has done more for human rights than any other force on earth.

2. T F All human beings should be treated with respect.

3. T F Jesus was concerned only with our souls, not our earthly condition.

4. T F Liberation theology fails to honour the gospel.

5. T F In Christ we lose our distinctive characteristics so that we are all equal.

6. T F There are times when we should forgo our rights.

7. T F Christians owe the state nothing.

8. T F Black people are inferior to whites because God decreed it.

9. T F God considers women to be of equal status with men.

10. T F The gospel challenges slavery at its roots.

Group Discussion

1. Discuss the value or otherwise of 'positive discrimination' in favour of minority groups.
2. Arrange a multicultural evening and ask what others find difficult with your culture.
3. Find out how Christians can support the work of Amnesty International.

Personal Assignment

1. Examine your personal attitude to people of a different race from yourself.
2. Pray for persecuted Christians.
3. Examine whether your attitudes to the opposite sex are being formed by the Scriptures or by your upbringing.

True or False

1.T 2.T 3.F 4.T 5.F 6.T 7.F 8.F 9.T 10.T

Employment

The Technological Revolution is changing the Western understanding of work.

Gone is the time when all but the favoured few had to work for their very existence, when to be unwaged meant almost certain death – or at least terrible destitution. Today we talk of the post-industrial society, of the virtual abolition of work as we have known it and of a booming leisure industry.

But there is another side to the matter. We aren't finding the transition easy. The millions of unemployed, often on meagre incomes and in deprived environments, don't greet this as a new day of creative opportunity. Instead, many are bitter, alienated, disillusioned and depressed. Saved from starvation maybe, but not from the loss of hope.

The Technological Revolution makes man the worker permanently redundant. Self-monitoring factories declare even the machine-minder obsolete. Unless the shop-floor worker can be retrained and relocated he has no future. Mass unemployment is inevitable – unless someone comes up with some bright ideas!

However, first we must comment briefly on the two dominant economic theories of our society as they affect employment.

1. Capitalism and Communism

a. Capitalism

Capitalism insists that the rich and the poor will always exist and should seek peaceful co-existence for their mutual benefit. The wealthy put their wealth to work to produce more wealth. The labourer generates this wealth and is rewarded with a living wage. In a free enterprise system, excess capital will be used to generate more jobs, and unlimited expansion of the economy is theoretically possible.

Capitalism has been strongly undergirded by the falsely-named 'protestant work ethic' which teaches that diligent work is a moral duty, whatever the job and the working conditions.

This ethic (actually a humanist one born out of the Renaissance) has been criticised on many grounds. For example:

- ☐ It tends to slot people into a role appropriate to their class, thus denying the opportunity for a person to 'break out'

- ☐ It uses people as units of labour rather than treating them as whole people. A person's identity becomes determined by what he does, rather than by who he is. Little wonder that the redundant worker feels such a loss of personal identity

Raw capitalism itself is open to abuse by sinful human beings. Alienation, inequality and hardship are the common lot of the worker in such a system. There are other problems:

- ☐ Untrammelled trust in the power of the free market means that many suffer at times of dramatic change, as with the Industrial Revolution and now the Technological Revolution

- ☐ Enterprise is commonly motivated far more by the financial benefit to the investor than by the benefit to society as a whole

- ☐ There is no honourable place for those dispossessed of their jobs. They are the failures of society and little effort is made to develop new work – the market motivation isn't there

- ☐ It creates a highly-stressed 'driven' society, with little place for rest, and the attendant virtues born out of 'time to consider'

b. Communism

Socialism seeks to tackle these issues by proposing a co-operative economic system in which the means of production is common ownership vested in the state. Communism goes much further by insisting that the means of distribution should also be state-controlled, thereby moderating the market to ensure a fair distribution to all.

Communism has achieved spectacular economic success in nations such as China, but has failed in Russia. Ideologically, its repression of the human spirit breeds despair and frustration, leading sooner or later to inevitable counter-revolution.

The weakness of communism is its implicit belief in the perfectibility of man outside of Christ and its utopian conviction that through revolution a new society will be born. Because it is idealistic, such societies have required repressive force in order to operate the theory.

Socialism also fails to take account of the inherent selfishness in sinful men and women. Its mammoth state industries have generally produced inefficient management and an undermotivated workforce.

Socialist systems exalt the worker and, like capitalism, over-identify a man with what he does.

Capitalism is broadly associated with the Conservatives (UK) and the Republicans (USA), while socialism/communism has been the political philosophy of the Labour Party (UK) and, to a lesser extent, of the Democrats (USA). In Britain the contrast has been vividly demonstrated in conflicting party policies of free enterprise and state ownership respectively.

Neither system has been able adequately to produce a society where there is full and satisfying employment. So is there a better way?

The Bible doesn't propose an economic theory but it does provide an approach to work which can dramatically change the face of labour.

2. The Biblical Doctrine of Work

The Bible's view of work has to be understood with reference to three other concepts: the Sabbath, service and salvation.

a. The Sabbath

Read Genesis 1. What did God do at the end of each day? See, for example, v25. Then notice from Genesis 2:1-3 what God did when he had finished creating the universe:

> *'By the seventh day God had finished the work he had been doing; so on the seventh day he ___________ from all ______ ________.'*
>
> (Genesis 2:2)

From these two passages we can draw certain principles:

1. Work is honourable

God did not consider himself above labour.

2. Work is good

Work should be of a kind whose product can be described as 'good'.

3. Work gives satisfaction

The worker should be able to contemplate and appreciate the worth of his labours at the end of each day.

4. Work should also involve rest

Work should be done to a rhythm which includes a day of rest every week.

5. Work should produce results

There should be a sense of completion about each week's work.

From the beginning, God intended our labours to be satisfying – a far cry from the view of working life as a necessary drudgery whose only respite is the weekend, and let's hope it's not raining! Consider also Psalm 127:1-2 and Ecclesiastes 5:10-12.

The Sabbath was created for the blessing of humankind (Mark 2:27). It was instituted as a day of rest and recreation, of fellowship and worship, of blessing our fellow human beings.

Honouring the Sabbath kept a check on commercialism with its attendant evils of greed, debt, stress, materialism and exploitation. Little wonder that desecration of the Sabbath brought the judgment of God upon Israel. See how Nehemiah dealt with the issue during the restoration of Jerusalem (Nehemiah 13:15-18).

A national Sabbath, as far as is practically possible, allows a society as a whole to recreate, so promoting national well-being and improved economic performance. 'Keep Sunday Special' isn't just a religious issue!

By Jesus' time, this blessing of God had been turned into a legalistic curse. Jesus restored a proper understanding of the Sabbath by his own approach to it.

He also saved us from dead works and put the Sabbath principle into our hearts. The primary emphasis under the new covenant is not on the observance of a day but on living all our days in the rest which comes from grace (Hebrews 4:1-11). This sets us free to enjoy the creation ordinance of one day's rest in seven and to make rest in God, not our daily labours, the source of our identity.

b. Service

In contrast to the modern world, the Scriptures do not force a divide between the sacred and the secular. Consequently, all work is a ministry to God and to our fellow-human beings. Sacrificial love is to mark our tasks. Such love will produce diligence, punctuality and excellence.

Both employees and employers are called to serve one another. Hence, there is a concern for each other's well-being. This abolishes the need for confrontation between workers and management and instead allows co-operation. It may lead to creating jointly-owned companies.

c. Salvation

The Fall brought a curse upon all creation and not least upon work. A new factor came into being (Genesis 3:17-19). What does Solomon call it (Ecclesiastes 2:17-23)?

Redemption lifts the curse (Galatians 3:13-14). This will not ultimately be seen until the new creation at Christ's return, but the principles of the new age are already operating. Our work should fit in with God's ultimate plan, which is:

> *'Through [Christ] to ________________ to himself ______*
> *____________, whether things ____ __________ or things ____*
> *____________.'* (Colossians 1:20)

We are to bring these principles to bear upon work.

1. They will make us examine the type of work we perform

Not just any work will do. Is the product truly beneficial to the human race, a good gift from God? Try to identify some products which you consider to be decidedly *un*helpful to society.

2. We will be concerned about the conditions we work under

Do they uphold the dignity of men and women? Or degrade them by putting them in a soul-destroying environment or one that is dangerous to their health, or in a job whose demands threaten their family life?

3. We will want the work to give opportunity for a person to express his creativity and individuality

This will enable a person to have pride in his job and feel he has actually produced something at the end of the day.

To summarise, the Scriptures teach a harmonious rhythm of work and rest, which is service to God and an expression of the process of reconciliation. It has none of the modern contradictions and conflicts.

3. Defending Work

The political polarities of Western societies drive those on the left to emphasise the *right* to work, while those on the right stress the *responsibility* to work. This is unfortunate because rights and responsibilities go hand in hand, for both workers and management.

a. The right to work

This term has taken on a particular meaning: the responsibility of governments so to order their policies that all members of society are granted the human right of paid employment.

Biblically, we cannot speak of the right to work but we can speak of the rightness, or appropriateness, of work. God gave Adam a responsible job in Eden:

> *'The Lord God took the man and put him in the Garden of Eden to ________ it and ________ ________ of it.'*
>
> (Genesis 2:15)

Constructive work, beyond nest-building, is something which distinguishes people from the animals. A government which by its policies denies this, lowers human dignity.

Furthermore, work should have its reward. This is much more than merely a pay-packet. It is unfortunate that our society has so limited the concept of reward. Job satisfaction needs to include a sense of achievement, of producing something worthwhile, of creative expression, of appreciation by others (Matthew 25:14-30) – nobody thanks the unemployed.

But the pay-packet *is* important! In 1 Corinthians 9:7-12 Paul argues that even preachers are entitled to some material reward for their labours (see also Luke 10:7; 2 Timothy 2:6).

The Scriptures command us:

> *'Do not withhold good from those who deserve it, when it is in your power to act.'*
>
> (Proverbs 3:27)

The sober fact is that, though the unemployed aren't starving, they are far from well-off and most don't have sufficient resources either financially or environmentally to live a life of creative leisure.

In fact, enforced idleness not only gives opportunity for dissipation but creates loneliness, boredom and lassitude through lack of stimulus. It also contributes significantly to the rising crime rate.

It is a poor, not to say perverse, leadership that cannot find anything for people to do! At the very least, it shows a lack of creative initiative unworthy of those elected to govern the modern economic state.

Christians have a responsibility to speak out on this issue.

b. The responsibility to work

The responsibilities of an employer are clear:

1. He must pay the labourer worthily

The employee needs a living wage commensurate with the work done, sufficient to keep him and his dependents in health and honour. Woe to the employer if he withholds it:

> *'I will come near to you for judgment. I will be quick to testify against . . . those who ______________ labourers of their ________.'*
>
> (Malachi 3:5)

2. He must provide a safe environment for his employees

Deuteronomy 22:8 reminds us of our responsibility for the safety of others.

3. The work conditions and hours should not grind the face of the poor

4. He must deal fairly with employees, as to the Lord

> *'Do not threaten them, since you know that he who is both their Master and yours is in heaven, and there is no favouritism with him.'*
>
> (Ephesians 6:9)

The worker must be taken on as a person, not merely as a unit of labour.

Workers, too, have responsibilities:

1. To serve wholeheartedly as to the Lord (Ephesians 6:5-7)

This includes showing proper respect for a boss together with enthusiasm and willingness when working. Those working for Christians should not take advantage of the fact (1 Timothy 6:1-2).

2. To work honestly and not steal (Ephesians 4:28)

3. To provide for their own family (1 Timothy 5:8)

Scripture has a specific command for those who are wilfully idle (2 Thessalonians 3:6-10):

> *'If a man will not ________, he shall not ______.'*
>
> (2 Thessalonians 3:10)

c. Trade unions and employers' federations

The trade union movement arose because of the failure of employers to observe biblical principles. Banding together to defend certain basic human rights was the only way. Unfortunately, the whole process – which started with the best motives – has led to a sharp economic and political division.

Should a Christian join a trade union or an employers' federation? The answer lies in balancing two passages of Scripture, both of which were written to Christians:

> *'I have written to you in my letter not to associate with sexually immoral people – not at all meaning the people of this world who are immoral, or the greedy and swindlers, or idolaters. In that case you would have to leave this world.'*
>
> (1 Corinthians 5:9-10)

> *'Do not be __________ together with ____________________ .*
> *For what do righteousness and wickedness have in common?*
> *Or what fellowship can __________ have with ____________ ?'*
>
> (2 Corinthians 6:14)

One passage tells us to stay in the world, the other to come out. We are to be involved in the world and its affairs as salt and light (Matthew 5:13-16), but not to be compromised in our testimony by that involvement. In particular, a Christian must not be yoked to an unbeliever. This applies to covenantal relationships where we become dubbed with the other person's values and actions.

The issue then has to be decided on merit. How much commitment is required? Is there a real say? What is the strike policy? Can I exercise my Christian conscience?

Believers have vital contributions to make in industrial relations. Indeed, it would help if our divinely-given wisdom dominated! Blessed are the peacemakers.

4. Creating Work

Many things need doing in our society which will not naturally attract capitalists motivated only by profit. The government could, by redirecting part of the nation's wealth, create jobs which may not be strictly of economic necessity, but neither are they a mere playing at work by creating artificial jobs in local government.

For example, we could as a nation begin to clear up some of the mess of our past 'achievements' – derelict ground, inner city wastelands, spoilt countryside, defunct architectural monstrosities.

We can embark upon building houses for people instead of expecting people to fit economic units of accommodation. We might also build fine parks, elegant architectural testimonies to a generation with hope, new cultural resources. Our heritage could be given a face-lift. Our roads could be dramatically improved.

In the caring areas we could provide research and resources for the growing numbers of elderly and disabled people in our society. We could create real opportunities for deprived youngsters. Our caring professions could be properly staffed without that necessarily meaning wasteful inefficiency.

We could invest in leisure facilities for all. Craftsmanship could be revived as true art. Educative leisure could enhance the lives of many. Even tourism could be developed as a worthwhile industry instead of an offering of over-priced trash. Think of some more ideas.

Believers should put pressure on the government to take initiatives in creating worthwhile jobs, but the church should also take initiatives of its own, not least taking advantage of government funding where possible – provided there are no positively anti-Christian strings attached.

This is part of the church's care for the needy in society and shouldn't be seen as peripheral to the gospel. We should consider projects like:

- ☐ Drop-in centres for the unwaged
- ☐ Initiating projects for the good of the community
- ☐ Helping the unwaged put together CVs, application forms, coping with interviews
- ☐ Motivating those who have lost motivation
- ☐ Using unwaged Christians in the charitable service of the gospel

☐ Helping the unwaged obtain their social security benefits

☐ Providing educational facilities for those who need retraining

☐ Organising pressure groups on local councils and government to do something about the problems

☐ Helping wives and mothers to develop home- and community-based employment which keeps them in touch with their children and offers creative outlets for their talents – see Proverbs 31:10-31

'Whatever your hand finds to do, do it with all your__________.'
(Ecclesiastes 9:10)

****

Lesson 3

Employment

True or False

1. T F Capitalism is better than communism at producing a society where there is full and satisfying employment.
2. T F We should not work seven days a week.
3. T F The worker should be able to appreciate the worth of his labours at the end of each day.
4. T F The Fall brought a curse upon work.
5. T F There is nothing in the Bible to indicate the need for a harmonious rhythm of work and rest.
6. T F Unemployment undermines a person's sense of self-worth.
7. T F So long as it is work any job will do, whatever the product.

8. T F Employers should treat their employees fairly.

9. T F Employees working for Christians may turn up when they want and do what they like.

10. T F Christians can do a lot of good in industrial relations.

11. T F Unemployment is none of the church's business.

Group Discussion

1. Discuss the value of the work that each of you do.

2. Assess what your church is doing about unemployment.

3. Obtain information that will be of use in advising the unemployed.

Personal Assignment

1. Examine your own attitudes to your job, if you have one. Are they pleasing to the Lord?

2. Write down a report of your week's work as your boss might see it.

3. Assess your leisure activities. Are they worthwhile and recreative?

True or False

1.F 2.T 3.T 4.T 5.F 6.T 7.F 8.T 9.F 10.T 11.F

Sexuality

None of us can answer the question, 'Who am I?' without taking our sex into account. Equally, we cannot divorce our character from our sexual relationships and habits. Sexuality cannot be put in a box marked 'Private' in the way many secular thinkers believe – what we are in this area affects every part of our lives.

There was a time when people understood this. You could find out what sex you were simply by standing in front of a mirror. Most people believed that sexual intercourse belonged exclusively within marriage, and society's laws were heavily weighted to keep it there. Those who transgressed were recognised as fornicators and adulterers; those who practised homosexuality were perverted. Men and women worked within the roles of their natural gifting to ensure their mutual survival.

In the past few decades, all that has changed. Sex before marriage seems to be the norm. Adultery is so commonplace that it destroys one in three marriages. Homosexuality and bisexuality are presented in our schools as legitimate options. Lust and masturbation are considered healthy.

Meanwhile, feminism has attacked wholesale the traditional relationship and role of men and women in society, leaving many people sexually confused.

What has happened?

1. Four Destructive Ideas

In the 1960s, secular forces which had been gathering strength for many decades suddenly burst on to the streets. The attack was devastating to traditional morality. It was spearheaded by four ideas.

a. 'Let it all hang out'

This was a popular catch-phrase. It was based on the theories of psychiatrist

Sigmund Freud – that our parents and the church put a fear of sexual expression into our lives at an early age. This, so the theories go, produces inner conflicts which make us neurotic. As this is bad for us, we should shake off those restraints and freely indulge our sexual desires as we wish – 'Let it all hang out.'

As a result, masturbation and sex outside of marriage suddenly become healthy. Self-control is a sign of psychological sickness!

Our response:

Although our parents may have passed on to us some unbalanced notions, the Bible teaches us to honour them and their basic teaching. What blessing awaits those who honour their parents (Ephesians 6:1-3)?

Read Ephesians 4:19, and notice what has caused people to give themselves to impurity: 'Having lost all *sensitivity*'. In other words, they don't fear God.

The answer to sexual lust is not self-indulgence, but a new heart:

> *'I will ____________ you from all your ____________________ and from all your ____________. I will give you a ________ __________ and put a ______ ____________ in you; I will remove from you your heart of stone and give you a heart of flesh. And I will put my ____________ in you and move you to follow my ______________ and be careful to keep my ________.'*
>
> (Ezekiel 36:25-27)

Self-control – being ruled by the Spirit – is the source of true liberty:

> *'Live by the ____________, and you will ______ ____________ the ______________ of the __________ ____________.'*
>
> (Galatians 5:16)

b. The naked ape

Evolutionary theory denies that God created the world. Instead, it teaches that all life developed from the simple to the complex, from the weak to the strong.

Men and women are no more than highly evolved animals and they have no moral responsibility before God. All their actions are responses to their environment with a view to keeping the human race going. So love and marriage are merely complicated animal rituals for reproductive purposes.

Our response:

The Bible teaches that men and women are a special creation, different from the animals:

> *'What is man that you are mindful of him, the son of man that you care for him? You made him a little lower than the ________ ________ and ________ him with ________ and ________.'*
>
> (Psalm 8:4-5)

We are responsible to a moral God – therefore the person who sins will die spiritually but the righteous will flourish. What happens to men and women when they act like animals (2 Peter 2:12)?

Marriage reflects God's love, not just a biological urge to reproduce. Read Ephesians 5:25-32. How are husbands to love their wives (v25, 28)? What do husband and wife become in marriage (v31)?

Children are the fruit of that union but not its primary purpose.

c. *Lady Chatterley's Lover*

The publication in 1960 of D.H. Lawrence's book *Lady Chatterley's Lover* effectively abolished censorship of the written word in Great Britain. It also popularised a philosophy known as Romanticism. (This is not the same as romance.)

Lawrence portrayed sex within marriage as frustrated. Passion – moist, earthy, warm sensuality – was to be found in an illicit relationship. Marital unfaithfulness could now be justified in the search for passionate love.

Our response:

The Bible does not portray sexual faithfulness as dull, unadventurous frustration. Whatever the Song of Songs (Solomon) may have to teach us about the relationship between Christ and the church, it is primarily an exuberant celebration of passionate married love. It is a lie to teach that the choice is either a passionate affair or drab marital duty. Here's how the married couple in the Song of Songs describe their experience:

> *'Love is as strong as death, its jealousy unyielding as the grave. It burns like a blazing fire, like a mighty flame. Many waters cannot quench love.'*
>
> (Song of Songs 8:6-7)

d. All you need is love

Many theologians, wanting to avoid the extremes of legalism or licence, tried to find another way. So they abolished absolutes and came up with what is known as the 'situation ethic'. This states that we cannot know what is right and wrong until we face a specific situation, and every situation is unique. The one guiding principle we have is love.

So, for example, if it seems loving to sleep with your unmarried partner, then it must be right.

This sounds noble, except that most people understood love to mean 'enjoyment' – or self-indulgence. One result is that many people now equate sex with love. They then become disillusioned with the latter when the former isn't too good. Many become sexually promiscuous in a desperate search for love through sex.

Our response:

The love of God is not self-gratifying; it is sacrificial. Read 1 John 4:7-11. The situation ethic cheapens love.

Although the Bible is opposed to legalism, nowhere is love set against the law. Love is the right way to fulfil the law:

> *'He who loves his fellow-man has fulfilled the law. The commandments, "Do not commit adultery," "Do not murder," "Do not steal," "Do not covet," and whatever other commandment there may be, are summed up in this one rule: "________ ________ ________________ as yourself." Love does no harm to its neighbour. Therefore ________ is the ________________ of the ______.'*
>
> (Romans 13:8-10)

The situation ethic attempts to find an intellectual solution to the dilemmas of life. It takes no account of the possibility of prayer or of divine intervention. All its so-called new morality has provided is an intellectual justification for the old immorality!

2. The Fruits of Sin

We reap what we sow (Galatians 6:7-8). Is not the following a fair description of what has happened as a result of these destructive ideas?

> *'There is ______ ______________________, no __________, no acknowledgement of God in the land. There is ________ __________, __________ and ____________, _____________ and __________; they break all bounds, and _____________ follows bloodshed. Because of this the land mourns.'*
>
> (Hosea 4:1-3)

a. Sexually transmitted diseases have become rife

Apart from traditional syphilis and gonorrhoea we have recent epidemics of genital warts and herpes, widespread non-specific urethritis, increasing incidence of cervical cancer and now the killer disease AIDS. We can't say we weren't warned!

Where do the paths of the adulteress lead (Proverbs 2:16-19)?

Many believe that Proverbs 5:11 is a reference to the ravages of syphilis. Certainly in Romans 1:27 we are told that homosexual practices carry a price. This may well include disease. (Though AIDS is not a 'gay plague' we cannot discount the plain fact that the disease spread into the Western world through homosexual promiscuity. This doesn't mean that homosexuals should be singled out for special attack, because AIDS, like other sexually transmitted diseases, is spread through promiscuity – and that is the responsibility of society as a whole.)

Here is God's assessment of the immoral person:

'A man who commits ______________ lacks judgment; whoever does so ______________ himself. __________ and ______________ are his lot, and his __________ will never be wiped away.'

(Proverbs 6:32-33)

b. Family life is being destroyed

Countless families are unnecessarily wrecked each year as a result of adultery. Nobody can compute the misery caused to innocent partners and their children – depression, delinquency and drug-addiction can often be traced to sexual betrayal. The cost to society is more than economic; our very fabric is at stake.

c. Child abuse

Child abuse is an inevitable consequence of worshipping sex as a god. The Old Testament fertility rites led to the sacrificing of children to the god Molech. We do this today by indiscriminate abortion and by sexual abuse of children. God is very angry about this. Read Psalm 106:37-40.

3. The Way Back

a. The faults of traditional morality

The church undoubtedly got it wrong on many occasions in the past. Often sex was wrongly contrasted with spirituality (this idea has secular rather than biblical origins). In a desire to avoid lust, the church was apt to condemn passion in marriage – 'Have sex if you must, but don't enjoy it!'

Often, too, the prohibitions were presented with a harsh spirit rather than with grace. And that tempts people to rebel. So we need to repent of wrong attitudes towards sex and to receive our sexuality as a beautiful, enjoyable gift from God.

b. As it was in the beginning

> *'God created man in his own image, in the image of God he created him; ________ and ____________ he created them.'*
>
> (Genesis 1:27)

Sexual identity comes from God. Therefore we should accept our own bodies and sexual natures with thanksgiving.

Read Genesis 2:23-25. Marriage and sexual intercourse was given as a gift before the Fall – Adam and Eve neither sinned nor lacked spirituality when they made love.

Sexual perversion means abusing the way God intended it to be. Hence the following – among other, less well-known sexual perversions – are all condemned in Scripture as contrary to his will:

☐ fornication – sex before marriage (1 Corinthians 7:2)

☐ adultery – sex with someone other than your spouse (Exodus 20:14)

☐ incest – sex with a near relative (Leviticus 18:6)

☐ prostitution – sex for hire (Proverbs 23:26-28)

☐ bestiality – sex with an animal (Exodus 22:19)

☐ homosexuality – sex with someone of the same gender (Leviticus 18:22)

God's will with regard to sex may be summed up as: *One man joined to one woman to be one flesh for one life.*

c. Particular implications for homosexuality

Homosexual practice is a sign of a God-forsaken society. Read Romans 1:21-27. Why did God give them over to these things (v21, 23)?

Homosexual desires arise from the failure of parents to provide their children with proper role models and love. This is sometimes due to a dominant mother/weak father syndrome, sometimes to the absence of a father at the crucial puberty years. Lesbian tendencies develop most often out of hatred or fear of men engendered by experiences of violence, sexual abuse or neglect. There is little or no evidence to support genetically predetermined homosexuality.

The effects of poor parental role-models can be lovingly remedied in the church. So-called 'Christian homosexuality' (in other words, faithful homosexual 'marriage') is not a biblical option.

Read 1 Corinthians 6:9-11. What will the wicked not inherit? Are the Corinthians still behaving in the same way as in the past? What has happened to them?

Homosexuals who come to the Lord should adopt a chaste, celibate lifestyle and be encouraged to seek the Lord for a healing of their homosexual orientation. Some will enter heterosexual marriage as a result, others will elect to remain single. All are called to freedom from the past.

d. The issue of masturbation

In spite of strong statements voiced by the church through the centuries, nowhere does Scripture condemn masturbation as such. Nor is there any suggestion that it makes one blind, senile or spotty! However, it is an inadequate use of the sexual gift – sex turned in on itself. If regular, it suggests a lack of self-control (one aspect of the Spirit's fruit – Galatians 5:22-23) and may become a real bondage. If accompanied by lustful fantasies, it is a cause of sin.

The words of Jesus in Matthew 5:27-30 are relevant to this issue. He tells his followers to deal firmly with any practice that causes them to sin. Without minimising this, we do well to remember that there are human activities with far more devastating consequences than masturbation, such as gossip-mongering, anger and pride.

e. Single for Jesus

Paul has positive advice in 1 Corinthians 7:32-35 as to what to do with sexual energy, especially for single people: Serve the Lord with all your strength! It is perfectly possible to live a sexually pure life while single without frustration or regret. We need to promote this as a positive option.

Let it be known that virginity is *not* an adolescent complaint. Chastity is honourable. Marriage is beautiful. Thus can we show the world the way back to true and fulfilled sexuality that is pleasing to God and a blessing to us.

f. Be clean

Whatever our past, we are called by God to demonstrate the wisdom and joy of living his way in the midst of a confused, sinful world. However, we may have past sin to be dealt with.

All sexual sin can be forgiven. Repentance and confession brings release from both actual and felt guilt. This is the good news in Jesus Christ and we need to share it unashamedly. Read Psalm 51; it is David's repentance after he had sinned sexually. God heard his prayer.

****

LESSON 4

Sexuality

True or False

1. T F Sexual restraint is unhealthy.
2. T F The answer to sexual lust is not self-indulgence, but a new heart.
3. T F Immorality spreads disease.
4. T F Christians should only have intercourse out of necessity, not for enjoyment.
5. T F God's will regarding sex is: One man joined to one woman to be one flesh for one life.
6. T F Homosexuality is something to be left behind as much as theft or lying.

7. T F Jesus had nothing relevant to say about masturbation.

8. T F Chastity is honourable.

9. T F Some sexual sins are too bad to be forgiven.

Group Discussion

1. Take some time together to pray purity into one another's lives.

2. Discuss ways of promoting Christian sexual values among young people.

3. Discuss how we should respond to homosexuals, particularly in the light of the AIDS crisis.

Personal Assignment

1. Check your bookshelves, newspapers, TV viewing habits. Are they sexually pure?

2. If you are married, discuss with your partner the quality of your sexual life.

3. If you are single, examine your lifestyle to see if you are finding fulfilment in serving the Lord.

True or False

1.F 2.T 3.T 4.F 5.T 6.T 7.F 8.T 9.F

Marriage

Marriage/family is one of the five major social institutions necessary for a stable and productive society (the others being economy, education, law/government and religion). Yet it has been the target of major attacks in recent years – one in three marriages fails in the Western world.

Behind that statistic lies the tragedy of broken homes – hurt children, shattered dreams, betrayed trust, financial catastrophe and emotional illness. If ever there was a need for restoration it is here!

The factors behind the current sexual chaos have also undermined the concept of marriage. Some have given up the idea and opted for just living together so long as the feeling lasts. Over half of those who do marry have preferred a register office wedding. In 1980, thirty-five per cent of marriages were remarriages – our society is replacing lifelong monogamy with consecutive polygamy. Yet most people still believe in the 'ideal' of Christian marriage.

1. The Origin of Marriage

a. God's creation

Marriage is God's idea, not people's. This is contrary to the 'social contract' type of theory, which suggests that it evolved for economic and reproductive reasons.

> *'The Lord God said, "It is ______ ________ for the man to be __________. I will make a ____________ suitable for him." '*
> (Genesis 2:18)

The Lord created marriage to meet our inner need for fellowship. Loneliness was something alien to the Godhead. So the Lord acted to ensure that Adam was not lonely. Love, then, is the primary reason for marriage; reproduction is the fruit.

Read Genesis 2:21-25. What, according to verse 24, are the three things that constitute a marriage?

Ezekiel 16 gives us insight into how marriage was viewed:

> *'When I looked at you and saw that you were old enough for love, I spread the corner of my garment over you and covered your nakedness. I gave you my solemn oath and entered into a covenant with you.'*
>
> (Ezekiel 16:8)

b. Reaffirmed by Jesus

In a world of widespread divorce and immorality, Jesus unambiguously reaffirmed the creation order. Not only did he perform his first miracle at a wedding (John 2:1-11) but he made a number of significant statements, of which this is typical:

> *'Haven't you read . . . that at the beginning the Creator "made them male and female", and said, "For this reason a man will leave his father and mother and be united to his wife, and the two will become one flesh"? So they are no longer two, but one. Therefore what God has joined together, let man not separate.'*
>
> (Matthew 19:4-6)

What argument does Jesus use here to support marriage? And why does he say that men and women should not break up marriages?

c. The spiritual dimension

Marriage is an earthly institution, to meet our need for companionship and mutual support and to provide a secure framework for raising children. That's why there will be no marriage in heaven – it won't be necessary (Mark 12:24-25).

There is, however, another dimension to it. Marriage is a visual aid to demonstrate the relationship between Christ and the church (see Ephesians 5:22-33). This doesn't make marriage a sacrament but it does give it spiritual significance, especially when two believers marry.

2. The Importance of Covenant Faithfulness

We have noted from Ezekiel 16 that God enters a marriage covenant with his people. What was the sin which the Lord most often accused his people of (see, for example, Hosea 1:2; 4:12)?

Our covenant-God calls us to be faithful to our spouses. Spiritual blessing is directly linked with this (see Malachi 2:13-16).

The idea of a binding covenant isn't just an option. Without it, however informally made, a relationship cannot be called a marriage. 'Living in sin' is still the correct description of an uncovenanted sexual relationship.

Some Christians would maintain that a couple who have never been through a civil or religious ceremony may nonetheless be considered married in God's sight if the following are true:

☐ They have set up home together in such a manner as to make it very difficult for them to divide it into his and hers

☐ They consider themselves to be joined as though they were husband and wife

☐ They have expressed a meaningful, two-way commitment to stick together through thick and thin, and generally made that known to their friends

☐ They are interdependent in most areas of their lives

If such couples become believers there is much to be said for their ratifying their relationship before God.

3. The Grounds for Divorce

It is a sad fact of life that marriages break down for one reason or another. However, we must beware of becoming blasé about divorce. How does the Lord feel about it?

' "*I ________ divorce," says the Lord God of Israel.*'

(Malachi 2:16)

a. Divorce permitted

The Old Testament permitted divorce (Deuteronomy 24:1-5). The alternative would have been desertion, possibly sharing two partners, terrible insecurity for the children and the innocent party. Divorce is a merciful and realistic provision for regulating the results of sin.

b. The debate in Jesus' day and his ruling

When Jesus walked the earth there was a heated debate taking place over the grounds for divorce. It turned upon the meaning of 'something indecent' (Hebrew *ervah-dabhar*) in Deuteronomy 24:1. The question related both to the legal right of divorce and to the status of the divorced persons, especially if, as was usually the case, one or other wished to remarry. Would remarriage be adulterous?

The conservative rabbi, Shammai, argued that the words meant 'adultery'. His honourable desire was to reduce the number of divorces taking place for minor reasons, such as a woman losing her looks or being a poor cook. However, his exegesis was bad. The words cannot mean adultery because the passage in question presupposes remarriage – and the death penalty was prescribed for adultery (Leviticus 20:10-16), thus making remarriage impossible!

The other rabbi, Hillel, argued correctly that the words meant a fault other than adultery. However, in so doing he shifted the focus away from God's hatred of divorce to its being a matter of human rights. This opened the door to easy divorce and thus undermined the sanctity of marriage.

Jesus was drawn into the debate in Matthew 19:1-9. He goes straight for the root issue:

> *'Moses permitted you to divorce your wives because your ____________ were ________ . But it was not this way from the beginning.'*
>
> (Matthew 19:8)

He then makes a statement about the status of those who would divorce and remarry. He is not, as such, limiting the grounds on which people may divorce. As today, divorce was permitted for all manner of reasons. The question is rather: What so ends a marriage that divorce and remarriage can take place without implicating the innocent party in adultery?

Jesus replies, '*Porneia*'. That is the Greek word translated 'immorality' or 'marital unfaithfulness'. The term includes adultery *(moicheuo)* but extends to accommodate sexual abuse, perversion, homosexuality, prostitution and possibly gross flirtation and desertion (the latter certainly if there is another person).

This subject was a 'hot potato' and engaged Jesus in considerable discussion. Mark records a slightly different conversation, though on the same occasion (Mark 10:1-12). To the question, 'Is it lawful for a man to divorce his wife?' Jesus replies, in effect, 'Yes, of course it is. But the fact that something is permitted in law doesn't necessarily make it right or good. Divorce is a sign of something joined by God being broken by man. Don't do it. But if you do divorce [we take it to mean on weak "Hillel-type" grounds] and remarry then you will be committing adultery.'

This is consistent with Jesus' teaching in the Sermon on the Mount where he again attacks the view that provided you do it correctly, divorce (and remarriage) is perfectly acceptable (see Matthew 5:31-32). The divorced woman referred to here must be understood to be one who was divorced for reasons other than *porneia*. Luke 16:18 should be interpreted in the same way.

To summarise: Jesus is gunning for the guilty parties, those who would behave immorally *(porneia)* and those who would divorce their spouses for trivial reasons. They are hard-hearted. In their desire for public self-righteousness, many were using the excuse of 'marital incompatibility' in order to cover their real desire, which was to marry someone else without actually first committing adultery.

Jesus says, 'You can't do that. Unless you do what is in your heart [Matthew 5:27-28] and actually commit adultery, your original marriage still stands in the sight of God, even though you go through a formal divorce!'

In other words, what ends a marriage before death is not divorce but *porneia*, and only *porneia*. And *porneia* is sin.

This was devastating news. The only way to change partners was to commit adultery, and that was sin anyway! Little wonder the bemused disciples said,

'If this is the situation between a husband and wife, it is better not to marry' (Matthew 19:10). You are stuck with each other for life! 'That's right!' says Jesus.

c. Apostolic applications

The rest of the New Testament reinforces the sanctity of marriage. For example:

> *'Marriage should be ________________ by all, and the marriage bed ________ ________, for God will judge the adulterer and all the sexually immoral.'*
>
> (Hebrews 13:4)

Sexual immorality abounded in pagan society and questions inevitably arose which needed guidance. Paul answers some of these in 1 Corinthians 7:

1. Is it worth marrying?

Yes, he says, and you should not deny each other sexually. Your bodies belong to each other. I wish everyone was free to be unmarried and devoted to the Lord, as I am. But if you haven't the gift, then do have a sexually fulfilled marriage (v1-9).

2. Should Christians change partners after a few years if someone else comes along?

No, says Paul. If you have marital problems, work them out. If you can't, then remain separate until you are ready for reconciliation, but you mustn't marry someone else. It goes without saying that you mustn't commit *porneia* (v10-11; compare 6:13-18).

3. What's the situation if a Christian is married to a non-Christian?

Essentially the same, Paul declares. Your marriage is holy in God's sight, your children are spiritually legitimate and you may well get your partner saved. So don't divorce on grounds of spiritual incompatibility. But if your unbelieving partner deserts you (probably for someone else), then the marriage bond is broken. Conversion doesn't change your situation. It changes your character and your response to the situation (v12-24).

4. In our present crisis, is it wise to marry?

Don't panic when things look tough, Paul counsels. The temptation is to make hasty and foolhardy decisions, like getting divorced or rushing into marriage. I think, he reasons, you would be best to remain as you are. But if you are a virgin and really want to marry, that's OK. However, there's a lot to commend being single, especially when times are hard – not least, you can serve the Lord with all your heart. Consider it a positive option (v25-35).

5. How does this apply if our parents arranged the marriage and 'engaged' us some years ago?

Do you want to marry her? Then it is no sin to do so, in spite of the stresses of the times. But if you are happy as you are, that is the better course (v36-38).

6. What about widows?

Marriage, Paul points out, is intended to be lifelong (only *porneia* breaks it before death). But when a husband dies, a woman is free to marry again. But I think, he says, that normally she will be happier if she remains single (v39-40), unless she is a younger widow (1 Timothy 5:3-16).

4. Grounds for Remarriage?

a. Christians disagree

Many argue that only death ends a marriage, and that therefore bereavement provides the only non-adulterous grounds for remarriage.

This position is laudable in its desire to uphold the sanctity of marriage but it fails to do justice to either the underlying issues or the actual text of Scripture. In fact, it actually makes the Scriptures contradict one another.

It also raises an enormous number of pastoral problems. For example, do you tell a recently-converted thirty-year-old man and wife with three children to separate because it is his second marriage, the first having ended when he was nineteen? This is not an uncommon problem. If they refuse, do you say that have not repented? Do you not allow them into church membership?

Or what about the attractive twenty-three-year-old secretary who was deserted by her husband in favour of another woman a couple of years ago? She is now divorced. Is she to spend the next sixty years in solitude as payment for someone else's sin?

Not surprisingly, the world has been scandalised by such callousness on the part of the church. Compromises such as 'blessing' the second marriage only serve to demonstrate how unreal this is.

b. Clarifying the position

Biblically, and legally, divorce always permits remarriage. The question is simply whether any given remarriage will be adulterous and therefore contrary to the will of God. The answer depends on the grounds over which a couple divorced.

If *porneia* kills the marriage and divorce is in effect a decent burial, it follows that the innocent party is free, as in bereavement, to contemplate remarriage without committing adultery in the process.

The one guilty of *porneia* has committed adultery in any case and remarriage will automatically be adulterous.

A remarriage following divorce for incompatibility will also be adulterous.

c. What about conversion?

'If anyone is____ __________, he is a _____ ______________;
the _____ has ________, the _____ has ________!'

(2 Corinthians 5:17)

New birth means new life, and new life means new lifestyle. Whatever our sinful past, we must now change (1 Corinthians 6:9-11).

Some consequences of our past may have to be faced up to. For example, Paul could never undo the fact that he had persecuted the church and caused the death of Christians before his conversion. An unmarried mother cannot get rid of the child born to her out of wedlock.

If, before our conversion, we divorced and remarried in such a way that the Bible declares our present marriage to be adulterous, what can we do? Surely the answer is to express sorrow before God for the sin, then to ask him for grace and mercy to bring good out of bad and to bless the present marriage. Normally in these circumstances it is neither practical nor right to divorce again. Deuteronomy 24:1-4 forbids a second divorce in order to remarry a former spouse.

d. A new standard

God's people must lead the way in demonstrating God's perfect will with regard to marriage. Society desperately needs role-models of passionate fidelity if it is to be saved from total disaster.

That standard will challenge existing ways, not with a set of restrictive laws but with the power of the grace of God. It will show what love is really all about. Faithfulness will be seen to be so fulfilling that coveting the neighbour's wife will become the rarity rather than the norm.

****

LESSON 5

Marriage

True or False

1. T F Stable marriage is vital for society's well-being.
2. T F Marriage evolved because children needed looking after.
3. T F Marriage is a visual aid to demonstrate the relationship between Christ and the church.
4. T F A binding covenant is the key to marriage.
5. T F The Bible totally forbids divorce.

6. T F The rabbi Shammai said you could divorce your wife if she burnt the toast.

7. T F Human rights is at the root of the divorce issue.

8. T F Jesus taught that, while marriage should last a lifetime, it can be ended if there is immoral behaviour by one partner.

9. T F Sexual unfaithfulness and death are the two things that end a marriage in God's sight.

10. T F A Christian should not divorce his or her non-Christian partner on the grounds of spiritual incompatibility.

Group Discussion

1. Discuss how you would communicate Christian marriage standards to young people.

2. Discuss what counsel you would give to a woman whose husband regularly abused her and her children.

3. What advice would you give to a couple living together who were now attending meetings of your church?

Personal Assignment

1. Bring your marital state (single or married) before God. Is everything as it should be?

2. Get to know the children of a divorced person.

3. Talk to a non-Christian about 'soap-opera' marriage values.

True or False

1.T 2.F 3.T 4.T 5.F 6.F 7.F 8.T 9.T 10.T

Life

It is incredible that any civilised country with a Christian heritage should authorise the wholesale slaughter of its children. Yet that is precisely what has happened in most Western nations.

In Great Britain, since the passing of the Abortion Act in 1967, nearly three million babies have been legally and scientifically put to death before seeing the light of day. The womb is the most dangerous place to live in today's society – a child has a one in five chance of being killed at its mother's behest. Recent figures in Britain stand at a hundred and seventy-two thousand per annum, or one every three minutes.

During the same period the incidence of child abuse has increased dramatically, despite predictions that there would be fewer unwanted children.

Meanwhile, morally questionable experiments on human embryos continue, and at the other end of the scale the pressure is on for legal permission to assist people in taking their own lives – voluntary euthanasia.

In the words of Francis Schaeffer, 'Whatever happened to the human race?'

1. Abortion – the British Legal Position

In 1861 the Offences Against the Person Act made abortion a felony punishable by life imprisonment. The 1929 Infant Life Preservation Act modified this so that a pregnancy might be prematurely terminated in order to save the life of a mother. Clearly, this recognised that the baby might die in the process, but it was not the intention to kill it. This act was widened in the 1938 Bourne Case, when the phrase 'life of the mother' was deemed to include acute mental anguish as the result of a pregnancy arising from rape.

As late as 1948 the Declaration of Geneva stated: 'I will maintain the utmost respect for human life from the time of conception' – a view reflected in law to that date.

All this changed dramatically in 1967. David Steel's abortion bill has been described as naïve, clumsy and sinister. Whatever his intentions, it effectively opened the door to abortion on demand. The wording is such that abortion is now 'no longer an offence' provided certain criteria are met. These criteria are:

1. *Risk to the life of the mother*

2. *Risk of injury to the physical or mental health of the mother*

3. *Risk of injury to the physical or mental health of existing children*

4. *Substantial risk of the child being born abnormal*

5. *In emergency to save the life of the mother*

6. *In emergency to prevent grave permanent injury to the physical or mental health of the mother*

The 1990 amendments to the law now permit abortion up to birth in certain circumstances, although they are exceptional ones relating to grounds four and six. The same amendments reduced the limit for late abortion under grounds two and three from twenty-eight to twenty-four weeks. As most abortions are performed earlier, this makes little effective difference to the number of babies killed.

The majority of abortions are performed under the second of these criteria. The reason is simple – risk of injury is implicit in all pregnancy. As no parameters are given to quantify this risk, any woman may argue the case for an abortion. There is a risk. Therefore, I am entitled to abort this child!

The only restraining influence is the doctor's conscience. With over a hundred and fifty thousand abortions procured on this ground each year, that appears not to be very effective.

On average, less than ten abortions are carried out each year in cases of genuine danger to the life of the mother.

The argument that such a law would abolish back-street abortion has proved unfounded. These have remained constant, and in recent times have revealed a disturbing increase.

2. 'Business Arising'

The change in the law has spawned an industry of 'pregnancy advisory centres', that is, legalised private clinics whose only function is to kill babies for money.

This may seem undesirable, but the law produces other 'business arising' too.

Approximately twenty per cent of aborting mothers are left with some permanent physical damage. This may range from persistent infection, blood clots and perforation of the uterus right through to sterility. Abortion is not corrective surgery; it is an assault on the body.

Post-abortion suicidal tendencies, depression, emptiness and guilt are common. This can be a time-bomb when, twenty or thirty years later, the aborting mother attends the weddings of her friend's children and remembers that she had hers killed before birth.

The law has politicised the appointment of gynaecologists and senior medical staff. Those whose consciences don't permit them to perform indiscriminate abortion find it harder to obtain promotion on merit. Posts tend to go to those who have no such conscience.

The most common methods of abortion in Great Britain are vacuum aspiration and D & C (dilatation and curettage). Both involve the chopping up of a live and pain-sensing baby and then, where necessary, crushing his or her head to pulp with specially-designed forceps. It is a medical barbarity.

3. The Spiritual Issue

Are there any spiritual implications in all this? The church was largely silent in 1967, and many in society would say that is a good thing – let priests perform religion when we need it; leave us to run the real world.

But this is *God's* world and, as his children, Christians are responsible for how it is run.

a. The value of life

The Abortion Act is built upon the philosophy of evolutionary humanism, the view that all living creatures have developed deterministically from primeval chemical reactions.

As no more than sophisticated animals we have no absolute moral standards, there being no God. We must base our judgments on expediency, so that the race may survive. Indeed, today we have the power to determine our own evolutionary future. We may abort the unwanted and the deformed, manipulate genes to our convenience, encourage voluntary suicide in the worn-out. It's a new day for the human race!

This runs counter to the Word of God. Man is unique (Genesis 1:27):

> *'When I consider your heavens, the work of your fingers, the moon and the stars, which you have set in place, what is ______ that you are mindful of him . . . ? You ________ him a little lower than the ________________ beings and ______________ him with __________ and ____________.'*
>
> (Psalm 8:3-5)

Children seem to have a special place before God (see, for example, Matthew 18:5-6; Mark 10:13-16).

b. Life before birth

There is no scientific or medical doubt that a baby is a separate human being from the moment of conception, though there is debate over whether this should be defined as at the fertilisation of the ovum or at the subsequent implantation of the fertilised embryo in the womb. However, it is pure guesswork to suggest that the new human being does not receive a soul until the moment of implantation or later.

Because the unborn baby is a human being, abortion as it is currently practised is an abuse of human rights.

God works in partnership with our own activity in conceiving children (Ruth 4:13). This fact gives all human life a divine dimension that we tamper with at our peril.

We also know that the development of the child in the womb is more than the unfolding of a genetic programme. God is himself directly involved. Job, concerned that God seemed about to destroy him, reminds the Lord that it was he who put him together in the first place (Job 10:8-12). Note that Job had a 'spirit' when he was in the womb.

Clearest of all is the following:

> *'You created my inmost being; you knit me together in my mother's womb . . . . My frame was not hidden from you when I was made in the secret place. When I was woven together in the depths of the earth, your eyes saw my unformed body [literally 'embryo']. All the days ordained for me were written in your book before one of them came to be.'*
>
> (Psalm 139:13-16)

God determined our sex, physical characteristics, parents and genes. Even if no-one else observed us as human, he did.

Babies in the womb respond to outside stimuli. They can on occasions even respond spiritually. John the Baptist was filled with the Spirit from birth, but before that he leapt for joy in Elizabeth's womb when she met Mary, herself pregnant with Jesus (Luke 1:39-45).

c. The sacrifice of children

The ancient world worshipped a particularly vile god called Molech and child-sacrifice featured highly in the ritual. The appeasing of this god was related to the desire for good crops and many sons.

It was a practice which God hated (Leviticus 20:2-3).

> *'They ____________________ their sons and their daughters to ____________ . They shed innocent blood, the blood of their sons and daughters, whom they sacrificed to the __________ of Canaan, and the land was __________________ by their blood.'*
>
> (Psalm 106:37-38)

God made it abundantly clear to his servant Abraham that he did not actually require the sacrifice of his first-born son, Isaac (Genesis 22).

Today we sacrifice children to the same idols of material prosperity and sexual indulgence. The gynaecologist has become the priest of an ancient demonic religion. His altar is the operating couch, his acolytes the nurses, the knife is now sterile but no less deadly to the innocent child who today is denied even one breath of air or comforting suck at his mother's breast.

4. Christian Response

a. Defend the weak

Proverbs 31:8-9 says we are to 'speak up for those who cannot speak for themselves, for the rights of all who are destitute. Speak up and judge fairly; defend the rights of the poor and needy'.

> '________________ *the cause of the* ______________ *and*
> ________________ *; maintain the* __________ *of the* ______
> *and* ____________________ . ____________ *the* ________ *and*
> __________ ; ______________ ________ *from the hand of the*
> ____________ .'
>
> (Psalm 82:3-4)

We have a responsibility to argue the case for the unborn. And this includes the deformed. God's answer is *care*, not *kill*. What do you make of Exodus 4:11; Leviticus 19:14?

In whose interests is it to abort a deformed child? In any case, it isn't even possible to assess accurately who is deformed in the womb – and some tests may even *produce* deformity. And once we kill some because of their deformity, why not others later? And what of those who become deformed through mishap at or after birth – the disabled?

b. Care for the bereft

It's no use commanding a starving man not to steal food unless we also provide him with bread. In the same way, to advise a teenage girl not to abort her illegitimate baby, without providing all the help she needs, is callous. We will be in danger of Jesus' attack on the Pharisees (Matthew 23:4).

Love, practical support, a roof over her head, protection, advice, adoption advice – all need to be provided. What is the mark of true religion given in James 1:27?

c. Educate the ignorant

A good half of unnecessary abortions are carried out on married women. In many cases it is seen simply as a form of birth control. The double-think, euphemistic language ('disposing of foetal matter', 'terminating a pregnancy', 'just a blob of jelly'), pressurising and withholding of the facts are such that many people are in ignorance of what is going on.

We have a responsibility to educate, especially young people reared on a false notion that all that matters is their own right to enjoy life as they please:

> *'My people are destroyed from ______ ____ ____________.'*
>
> (Hosea 4:6)

5. Genetic Engineering

In 1961 the first tadpoles were cloned (genetically identical specimens grown from a single cell). The year 1962 celebrated the unravelling of DNA by James Watson and Francis Crick. In 1966 Robert Edwards cultivated human ova in a laboratory. By 1969 ova could be grown to a hundred cells. In 1978 Louise Brown was born – the first 'test-tube baby'.

Recently it was reported that a British scientist was experimenting in taking a cell-nucleus from his own body, inserting it into a human egg and implanting this into a monkey's womb to grow into a foetus. His aim: to kill both monkey and foetus and use the genetically compatible 'spare parts' of the baby to replace his own.

Equally grotesque experiments have been done on chimpanzees with a view to the possibility of homosexual men carrying pre-fertilised ova in their abdominal cavities, later to be delivered of the baby by Caesarean section. Similarly, it is possible by egg-fusion to give a lesbian couple guaranteed female offspring.

With some ten per cent of people unable to conceive and a further fifteen per cent having difficulty, it is understandable that we should seek to do something about infertility. However, what we do has to be governed by moral and spiritual considerations. Because these don't rank high among some geneticists, the only limit to what may be attempted is dictated by public opinion.

As those concerned for the sanctity of human life we Christians must pass comment.

Artificial insemination by the husband may be justified in some circumstances. However, the economically-determined practice of fertilising several ova and either disposing of or experimenting upon the unneeded ones should be discontinued. In fact, human fertilised ova should never be experimented upon – these are, after all, children in all but age.

Artificial insemination by donor divorces life-giving from love-making and brings a third, albeit anonymous, person into the marriage. Questions arise as to the legal status of the child and the psychological acceptance of the child by the stepfather. And there are increasing concerns about the genetic and health risks for society should widescale AIDS continue.

There are a growing number of acceptable ways of preventing and curing genetically transmitted diseases without the need for human embryo experimentation. And if only one per cent of abortions were discontinued, there would be enough babies available for adoption for all who are childless.

6. Euthanasia

The word 'euthanasia' means 'easy death' or 'mercy killing'. It is an emotive subject. How long do you let a suffering person go on living, especially when he or she wants to die? Isn't it charitable to put such people out of their misery with a fatal drug?

In an age when people live longer, doesn't it make economic sense to encourage non-productive members of society to terminate their lives in order to conserve resources for the younger generation?

Part of the problem today is that we can keep people alive much longer than previously. Pain itself shortens life, but that can now largely be alleviated. Life-support machines can sustain bodily functions almost indefinitely even though there is no hope of conscious recovery.

Easy death as a medical technique seems a neat solution to the problems raised by terminal illness.

But is it? Who is going to make the decision? The pain-ridden patient? Or relatives, shattered with grief or callously wanting to get Aunt Nellie's fortune? Or a central committee? Or the doctor whose training and responsibility it is to save life? Who would trust a doctor if you knew he had legal power to terminate your life? It is unwise to play God when you lack his attributes!

All positive killing of humans is murder in God's sight:

> *'You shall not murder.'*
>
> (Exodus 20:13)

Having said this, those who are obviously dying should be allowed to do so. Living corpses should not be sustained on machines – that does nothing for the dignity of human life. We should properly distinguish between saving life and merely prolonging the process of dying.

The best approach to dying lies nowadays in the *hospice movement* where, with a high staff-to-patient ratio and skilled counselling and drug administration, patients are able to die with dignity. Many Christians are actively involved in this movement. Such care for the dying is the final loving brush-stroke in the art of healing.

****

LESSON 6

Life

True or False

1. T F Most abortions are performed for convenience rather than because of genuine need.
2. T F People are not being told the whole truth about abortion.
3. T F A foetus is not really a human being.
4. T F The development of the child in the womb is simply the unfolding of a genetic programme.

5. T F Babies in the womb should have rights.
6. T F Society today sacrifices children to the idols of material prosperity and sexual indulgence.
7. T F It is a morally neutral thing to experiment on human embryos.
8. T F Artificial insemination by husband may have a place in certain circumstances.
9. T F Everyone over seventy should voluntarily take a suicide pill to ease the burden on tax-payers.
10. T F The Bible says, 'You shall not murder.'

Group Discussion

1. Discuss how you would counsel and help an unmarried pregnant woman who was contemplating an abortion.
2. How would you handle the statement, 'All deformed foetuses should be aborted'?
3. Discuss a strategy for educating the young people in your church and local schools on these issues.

Personal Assignment

1. Consider joining an organisation such as CARE or LIFE in order to support efforts to repeal the abortion law.
2. See whether you can't visit patients in your local hospice.
3. Join the spiritual warfare against 'Molech worship' when you pray.

True or False

1.T 2.T 3.F 4.F 5.T 6.T 7.F 8.T 9.F 10.T

The Poor

We live in a divided world. It is the world of the haves and the have nots, of the stark division between rich and poor, of the economic oppressors and the oppressed.

At a time when the techno-nations enjoy a wealth unparalleled in human history, over five hundred million people are starving to death and another one billion are suffering chronic malnutrition. Untold millions more struggle against the daily deprivation wrought by unending poverty – they are powerless, in poor health, lacking education, constantly weary and dying prematurely.

Earn £100 a week and your poor Two Thirds World counterpart will earn only £10. But things are not ten times cheaper for him. Your poor neighbour is in real terms often ten times worse off than you.

Or look at it this way. The USA uses only seventeen per cent of its disposable income on food. The other eighty-three per cent is spent on medicine, education, comfortable living and defence. But a nation like India has to spend no less than sixty-seven per cent of its disposable income on food, leaving only a third of what is a much less valuable sum anyway, available for everything else.

The problem is exacerbated in many developing countries because small élites often hold the majority of the nation's wealth. For example, in Brazil some five per cent of the population hold thirty-eight per cent of the wealth. In these countries a global process known as emisseration takes place with particular fierceness. (Emisseration is that process where the rich become both fewer and richer while the poor become poorer and more numerous. Disaster is inevitable if the process is not reversed.)

The International Monetary Fund was set up ostensibly to assist the funding of developing countries. However, because of the high interest rates, these countries have often been unable to pay off the loans. As a result they have had to borrow, at a rate of interest, in order to pay the interest on the first loan. Soon they can't pay this either and have to borrow again – at a rate of interest.

It is becoming impossible for some Third World countries ever to pay their debts. And what they *can* pay demands high taxation on the very people who should have received the benefit of the original loan. A fluctuation in the interest rates can mean death by taxation for those at the bottom of the social scale.

Nor is it simply possible for loan repayments to be waived. Such is the magnitude of the debt that this would have serious repercussions for Western economies. And indeed for our pensioners, as many pension schemes depend on overseas investment. We live increasingly in a global village.

Tackling the problem of world poverty is a major item for the agenda as we approach the twenty-first century. But it has only recently become part of the evangelical agenda. Why?

1. Reaction of Evangelicals

For most of this century evangelicals have taken very little interest in the plight of the poor. Part of the reason has been a sinful *middle-class complacency,* itself made possible by the acquisition of wealth gleaned from the poor of the world. Such an attitude would have earned the indignation of the prophets. Read what Amos has to say about it:

> *'They ____________ on the heads of the ________ as upon the dust of the ground and __________ ______________ to the __________________.'*
>
> (Amos 2:7)

(See also Amos 4:1-2; 5:11-12.)

There is also a *theological reason.* Towards the end of the last century there developed what became known as the 'social gospel'. This was a theologically liberal response to the view, born of 'education', that traditional biblical Christianity was no longer tenable. What was left for the church to do? Why, justify its existence by ministering to the needs of society.

Evangelicals, who had always done this as an expression of their faith, now reacted by putting the emphasis on holding to 'the truth once for all delivered to the saints'. They retreated *en masse* into their church services and began to decline.

The development of Christian Socialism further compounded this by bringing in a political element that many of the middle classes found unacceptable. This presents itself in a modern, more extreme form in many Third World countries with what is known as liberation theology – 'Christianised' revolutionary Marxism – as we saw in lesson 2.

Liberation theology redefines the gospel in socio-political terms. It seeks biblical support in the liberation of the Israelites from Egypt and the heroic death of the revolutionary, Jesus.

'Salvation' is thus redefined, being worked out in the struggle for economic justice against the exploitation of people by people; in the struggle for human dignity against political oppression of men and women by their fellow human beings; in the struggle for solidarity against the alienation of person from person; in the struggle of hope against despair in personal life.

Mere charitable action is viewed as an actual hindrance to the need for fundamental change in the political structures which create poverty. If necessary, violent means may be used to bring this about.

Needless to say, evangelicals have been extremely guarded about these developments, though a younger generation is less patient.

2. Biblical Viewpoint

What does the Bible have to say on these issues? Quite a lot! The biblical writers have none of our reticence in talking about money, and they certainly don't duck the issue of poverty.

a. Concern for the poor

God wants us to be concerned about the plight of the poor.

We have already noted the blunt prophecies of Amos which will not allow us to hide under a cloak of religion. What is true fasting all about? Isaiah gives the answer (see Isaiah 58:6-10):

> *'To loose the chains of ___________________ . . . to set the ___________________ free . . . to share your food with the ___________ and to provide the ________ _______________ with shelter'.*
>
> (Isaiah 58:6-7)

James defines the essence of practical Christianity to include care for the poor of the day:

> *'Religion that God our Father accepts as pure and faultless is this: to look after ______________ and ____________ in their ______________ and to keep oneself from being polluted by the world.'*
>
> (James 1:27)

And, in a most amazing statement, Jesus assesses the difference between the sheep and the goats, not on the basis of professed faith in him, but on the basis of who serves him by ministering to the needy (Matthew 25:31-46).

A significant part of Paul's apostolic ministry consisted in raising money in order to provide for famine relief. In 2 Corinthians 8 and 9 he reveals his heart in this. Note his answers to the following questions:

☐ What is the great motivation to give? (8:9)

☐ Do you have to be rich to give? (8:1-3)

☐ What is the measure of our reaping? (9:6)

☐ What is a sign of God's righteousness? (9:9)

☐ What else happens when we supply the needs of the poor? (9:12)

Although Jesus came seeking all people, his ministry had a significant impact among the poor (Matthew 11:5). The feeding of the five thousand and of the four thousand, though by no means famine relief, nonetheless tells us that Jesus was concerned with the whole person and not just the spiritual aspect. There is also a hint in the miraculous nature of his supply that our own care for the poor needs a charismatic dimension.

The parable of the Good Samaritan (Luke 10:25-37) defines our neighbour as anyone who crosses our path, regardless of colour, creed or country of origin. Paul sums it up:

> *'As we have __________________, let us do _______ to ______ ___________, especially to those who belong to the ___________ of _________________.'*
>
> (Galatians 6:10)

This keeps us from either doing nothing or trying to do everything. Real wisdom!

b. Freedom from covetousness

Materialistic philosophy dominates both the capitalist and socialist economic systems in our modern world. Jesus challenges the assumption that we should find meaning to life only in what can be seen and touched:

> *'Watch out! Be on your guard against all kinds of __________; a man's life does not consist in the ________________ of his ____________________.'*
>
> (Luke 12:15)

He went further and declared that it was extremely difficult for a rich person to be saved (see Luke 18:18-25). So, out of love for him, Jesus told the rich young ruler to sell all he had and to give it to the poor (Luke 18:22).

Covetousness is a curse. It can be the vice of a man with only five pence to his name. It is especially a threat to the affluent. The only way that a person with assets and the ability to make money can be an heir to the kingdom of God is by becoming a generous giver, especially to the poor (1 Timothy 6:17-19).

Paul gives some specific advice on how to give to the poor in 1 Corinthians 16:1-2. What is it? And what sort of giver does God like (2 Corinthians 9:7)?

c. Religion and politics can mix to provide a remedy

The Scriptures are always realistic, never idealistic. As we saw in lesson 2, Paul didn't attack slavery as such but nonetheless made it impossible for any true believer to continue treating his slaves as slaves (see Philemon 15-17).

The implications of this are tremendous. How, on that basis, could we ever cram the working classes into tenement housing, let alone keep anyone in economic, racial or political subjugation, once given the opportunity to do something about it?

However, whatever means we use to bring about social and political change, they must be *non-violent.* This is apparent from Jesus' words to Pilate in John 18:36. Our warring is in the spiritual realm, the home of the real powers (Ephesians 6:10-12). Prayer and proclamation can change a policy, or a government.

Does the Bible give us any economic clues beyond the charitable? Is there a godly way to arrange the economics of a society and, indeed, of a world so as to lessen the appalling divide? The answer is 'yes'.

1. The spirit of temperance

The malaise of the West is due in large part to worshipping the false god of mammon (money). Governments as well as individuals need to repent of this and temper their policies by the principle of wisdom found in Agur's prayer:

> *'Give me neither poverty nor riches, but give me only my daily bread. Otherwise, I may have too much and disown you and say, "Who is the Lord?" Or I may become poor and steal, and so dishonour the name of my God.'*
>
> (Proverbs 30:8-9)

This assesses the degree of wealth we should possess by its effect on the soul, not by our place in the league table of world economic growth. As a result, we will temper our growth and therefore our exploitation of the poorer nations. Maybe we will also seek to protect them from others more greedy.

It is this spirit of temperance which undergirded the Mosaic law and led to legislation to prevent gross extremes of wealth and poverty.

2. Sabbath-year emancipation (Deuteronomy 15:12-18)

This prevented 'class' from developing in the nation by giving employees, every seven years, the opportunity and the resources to set up on their own if they wished. In effect, it was a profit-sharing scheme on a national scale. The worker was a direct personal beneficiary of the economic growth.

3. Jubilee restoration (Leviticus 25:8-17)

The fifty-year lease system not only taught that men and women were but stewards of the Lord's earth; it also served to control property prices. These were determined by the genuine business potential of the land rather than by what people were willing to pay for it. Speculation was thus discouraged.

> *'Do ______ _______ ________________ of each other, but _______ your ______.'*
>
> (Leviticus 25:17)

4. Interest-free loans (Leviticus 25:35-38)

No money was to be made out of other people's poverty or misfortune. What a difference this would make to the modern world! An absence of high interest rates would transform society.

Our modern 'get rich quick on the stock exchange' mentality would have to go, of course. Maybe recent crashes on the markets are God's warning shots across the bows of the Bad Ship Enterprise. When enterprise is used to promote the good of the human race, especially of the deprived, God will bless it.

5. The release of debts by creditors (Deuteronomy 15:1-6)

There must surely come a time when we stop asking for our rightful dues from those who in any case cannot pay. And in many instances those poorer countries have helped make us rich in the first place.

> *'At the end of every seven years you must __________ _______.'*
>
> (Deuteronomy 15:1)

6. Direct provision for the poor (Leviticus 19:9-10; Exodus 23:10-11; Deuteronomy 10:16-19; 14:28-29)

Foreign aid needs to be increased – and provided with the necessary wisdom and safeguards to see that it reaches the right place and supplies appropriate technology. Great Britain has not reached the recommended minimum and in fact has now reduced its foreign aid.

The implications of economic temperance are worth discussing at personal, national and international levels. Herein lies hope for the future.

d. A new age

> *'You will always have the poor among you, but you will not always have me.'*
>
> (John 12:8)

This world is sinful and passing away. Today's economic system can be greatly alleviated by attention to biblical principles, but ultimately it is corrupt and must perish. Greed is deeply in the nature of men and women without God.

We seek to bless all people in our generation, but our hope is in the return of Christ and in the establishment of a new heaven and a new earth in which righteousness dwells. Then the nations will be truly healed (Revelation 22:1-3).

****

LESSON 7

The Poor

True or False

1. T F The majority of the poor are in that state because they haven't made the most of their opportunities.
2. T F Christians should promote violent political revolution in order to change the economic system.
3. T F Concern for the poor is part of the gospel.
4. T F We should regularly set aside money for the poor.
5. T F We should only help poor people if they are the same religion as us.

6. T F It is extremely difficult for a rich man to go to heaven.

7. T F The spirit of moderation should govern our acquiring of possessions.

8. T F The Scriptures forbid the charging of interest to the poor.

9. T F There will be no famine in the new heaven and the new earth.

Group Discussion

1. Discuss ways in which you think you could influence your Member of Parliament to promote biblical economic principles.

2. Discuss how you would convince a communist that Christian economics are more radical than those of Marx.

3. Research an area of poverty and implement some form of action to help deal with it.

Personal Assignment

1. Carefully examine your lifestyle with regard to possessions to ensure that you are free from idolatry.

2. Check that you are obeying Paul's principle of setting some money aside for the poor each pay-day.

3. Read a book about current Christian responses to world poverty.

True or False

1.F 2.F 3.T 4.T 5.F 6.T 7.T 8.T 9.T

LESSON 8

The Environment

One of the phenomena of the late twentieth century has been an upsurge of interest in the environment. Terms like ecological impact, global village, greenhouse effect, rain forest, ozone friendly and recyclable wastes have become part of everyday speech.

The colour is unmistakably Green – complete with its own Party and its own Peace, so that today no political agenda can afford to ignore 'green issues'. Meanwhile, manufacturers bend over backwards to convince us that they are producing 'environmentally friendly' products.

The concern is justified. Since 1800, the world's population has grown from an estimated one billion to nearly six billion people. This, and the combined effect of the agricultural, industrial and technological revolutions, makes us the most environmentally demanding species on earth. We consume renewable resources faster than they can regenerate. Our incessant demand for consumables converts non-renewable resources into pollutants that threaten the well-being of the entire ecosystem, including our own species.

Ecologists, and many in the New Age movement – that conglomeration of associated ideas relating to a more 'spiritual' approach to life, including a revived pagan veneration of Mother Earth – warn us that we must act swiftly and responsibly if we are to avoid disaster.

Christians aren't noted for being conservationists. Indeed, sometimes the whole problem is laid at our feet because Genesis 1:26-28 seems to justify violent exploitation of the earth. To this must be added the fatalism of those Christians who believe ecological disasters are a sign of the end times. Little point in cleaning the drains if the house is about to fall down!

Do we simply opt out and content ourselves with preaching the gospel, or do we have something positive to offer?

We begin with an optimistic view of our world:

1. The Doctrine of Providence

Providence is defined as God's mercy towards his creatures in providing us with all good things and in lessening the destructive effects of the Fall. There are four reasons why he does this:

a. He created the world

The world, indeed the universe, did not originate by chance but came into being, out of nothing, by the word of God:

> *'In the beginning God created the heavens and the earth.'*
>
> (Genesis 1:1)

> *'You are worthy, our Lord and God, to receive glory and honour and power, for you ____________ all things, and ____ ________ ______ they were created and have their being.'*
>
> (Revelation 4:11)

Although there is much scientific evidence to support the doctrine of creation, in the end we must accept the truth by faith – Hebrews 11:3.

The doctrine of creation opposes evolutionism, though it doesn't bar as a matter of interpretation the possibility of some restricted form of evolution. However, changeable scientific facts are a flimsy basis on which to base one's theology. Evolution – like the 'big bang' theory or 'punctuated equilibrium' – is essentially a statement of materialistic faith.

b. He sustains the world

God holds the universe together, and directs everything to the fulfilment of his purposes. 'The Son is the radiance of God's glory and the exact representation of his being, sustaining all things by his powerful word' (Hebrews 1:3). (See also Acts 17:24-28.) To whom was this addressed: Christians or non-believers?

This truth delivers us from the mistaken idea that God wound up a clockwork universe and then retired to let it run itself. He is intimately involved; the universe is held together not merely by impersonal subatomic forces but by the actual presence and power of God himself. Even the so-called laws of nature don't operate independently of God. He knows about the sparrows and the hairs of our heads – Matthew 10:29-30. Every leaf breathes with his life. (Pantheists falsely say he is the leaf, in other words, *everything* is God.)

c. He owns the world

Our heavenly Father owns everything:

> *'To the Lord your God belong the heavens, even the highest heavens, the earth and everything in it.'*
>
> (Deuteronomy 10:14)

> *'The __________ is the __________ , and ______________ in it.'*
>
> (Psalm 24:1)

See also Psalm 50:10-12 and 1 Chronicles 29:12-16.

In Psalm 115:16 we read, 'The highest heavens belong to the Lord, but the earth he has given to man.'

We have the use of God's world by his permission, not by right. Everything we have is on trust from him. Not surprisingly, he cares about how we steward the earth's resources. Environmentalism is, therefore, a Christian issue. However, it extends beyond just protecting the ecosystem; we are also responsible for how we behave, and for the *moral* use to which we put those resources.

d. He provides for the world

Our loving Father blesses humankind with great prosperity. Even though the world is under the curse of sin, it is still a good place in which to live:

> *'As long as the __________ endures, ___________________ and ______________ , cold and heat, _____________________ and ______________ , day and night will __________ __________ .'*
>
> (Genesis 8:22)

'You open your hand and satisfy the desires of every living thing' (Psalm 145:16). (See also Acts 14:16-17.) There is adequate food in the world to feed every mouth; its proper distribution is a moral issue before it is an economic one.

Our response to God's provision should be one of thanksgiving and deep gratitude. Romans 1:21 indicates that it is our refusal to give thanks to God for his providence that is the root cause of him giving us over to the consequences of idolatry.

> *'Give __________ in ______ ________________________, for this is ________ ______ for you in Christ Jesus.'*
>
> (1 Thessalonians 5:18)

God's providence not only gives us security (see Matthew 6:25-34), but it encourages us to affirm the essential goodness of the material world.

For example, it means we can eat what we like! Paul writes of 'things taught by demons', by which he meant legalistic practices which attribute a moral or spiritual value to denying sex and to restrictive dietary habits (see 1 Timothy 4:1-5). You are *not* what you eat. Jesus said it is not what goes into the mouth but what comes out of the heart that defiles a person (see Mark 7:15-23).

This counters New Age myths about Yin and Yang foods, or the supposed virtues of vegetarianism, or any other religiously-contrived diet. Moderation and self-control are Christian virtues, but you can't achieve moral excellence or personal worth by special diets. Only Jesus does this, through the cross and by our adoption as sons of God.

2. Responsible Stewardship

Genesis 1:26-28 cannot be interpreted as a mandate to treat the earth with irresponsible violence. Although addressed to a predominantly agrarian society, the Scriptures contain all the principles of conservation and environmental care. Here are a few examples from the 'case law' of Moses. Consider how they extend to our own society:

a. Animal rights

While there is no false sentiment attached to animals used for food and work – animals could be slaughtered, and if an animal harmed a human it would be put to death – there were a considerable number of laws for their well-being:

> *'Do not cook a young goat in its mother's milk.'*
>
> (Exodus 23:19)

This is a demand for humaneness in our treatment of animals. The milk that should nourish the kid and complete the mother's reproductive activity is not to be used for its death.

> *'On the seventh day do not work, so that your ox and your donkey may rest.'*
>
> (Exodus 23:12)

The Sabbath principle protects the entire environment from over-exploitation, including that of animals. It allows for renewal and sets a proper limit on unrestricted growth.

> *'Do not muzzle an ox while it is treading out the grain.'*
>
> (Deuteronomy 25:4)

A working animal is not to be deprived of the right to eat – its natural instinct and freedom – as it works.

b. Health and safety

Today we want laws protecting members of the public from danger caused by carelessness or inconsiderate greed. The principle was established in Deuteronomy 22:8: 'When you build a new house, make a parapet around your roof so that you may not bring the guilt of bloodshed on your house if someone falls from the roof.'

Likewise, our pollution control laws have a divine origin. Waste products are to be disposed of safely and hygienically:

> *'Designate a place outside the camp where you can go to relieve yourself. As part of your equipment have something to dig with, and when you relieve yourself, dig a hole and cover up your excrement.'*
>
> (Deuteronomy 23:12-13)

The simple modern application of this law is the single most important piece of preventive medicine a society can have.

There are many references in the Law to the importance of washing food, clothes and bodies, as well as treatment for mildews, the sterilising of drinking vessels and the quarantining of those with infectious diseases. Water could not be used if it was known to be polluted. The ban on eating scavenging animals or any creatures found dead by the wayside was a major protection against intestinal illnesses. See Leviticus 11 for some examples.

c. Conservation

We live in an age notorious for its relentless exhaustion of land, resulting in agricultural nightmares of dust-bowls and massive soil erosion. God commanded that the land should be allowed to rest and recover its fertility:

> *'For six years sow your fields . . . . But in the seventh year the land is to have a sabbath of rest.'*
>
> (Leviticus 25:3-4)

Fruit trees were not to be forced into early cropping, but allowed to mature (Leviticus 19:23-25). It is a caution about looking for a quick return at the expense of long-term considerations. This principle can be sensibly applied to over-fishing, deforestation or any excessive consumption of otherwise renewable resources. A quick buck is usually at the expense of the long-term stability of the environmental infrastructure.

Although designed for the benefit of the poor, Leviticus 19:9-10 warns against over-efficiency in harvesting. The demand to maximise output is a major cause of industrial and agricultural problems today.

d. Motivation

If these case studies supply the guidance, then the moral and spiritual transformation produced by the gospel is the dynamic. The parable of the rich fool recorded in Luke 12:13-21 touches the very root of our modern problem:

> *'Watch out! Be on your guard against all kinds of __________ ; a man's life does not consist in the __________________ of his _______________________ .'*
>
> (Luke 12:15)

James 5:1-8 contrasts vividly the rapacious rich with the one who works patiently with the rhythms of creation.

An attitude of consideration for our fellow-humans is at the heart of the gospel: 'Do nothing out of selfish ambition or vain conceit, but in humility consider others better than yourselves. Each of you should look not only to your own interests, but also to the interests of others' (Philippians 2:3-4). On this basis we will want to consider the wider consequences for others of all our activities, and temper them accordingly.

3. The End of the World

Earlier in this study we referred to the Fall. Adam and Eve's sin brought judgment on themselves and on the creation:

> *'____________ is the ______________ because of you; through painful toil you will eat of it all the days of your life. It will produce ____________ and ________________ for you.'*
>
> (Genesis 3:17-18)

This is the reason that there is more than a little truth in 'nature red in tooth and claw'. Things go wrong in this world; disasters occur, ecological and human. Jesus said that the last days (meaning the period from his ascension to his return) will be accompanied by famines and earthquakes. He described these as birth-pains (see Matthew 24:7-8). The apostle Paul takes up this idea in Romans 8:20-22. The environment is subject to futility, but we must see it in the light of a coming new creation.

New Agers and futurists like to see history as progress towards Utopia – a time when humanity will have put all things to rights. The Bible offers no such hope. Peter writes:

> *'The heavens will disappear with a roar; the elements will be destroyed by fire, and the earth and everything in it will be laid bare.'*
>
> (2 Peter 3:10)

What is promised is not the eternal conservation of the present order but a violent destruction at the coming of Christ, followed by a miraculous renewal of all things – the greatest environmental transformation imaginable!

> *'In keeping with his promise we are looking forward to a new heaven and a new earth, the home of righteousness.'*
>
> (2 Peter 3:13)

This glorious hope gives us no excuse for irresponsible activity in the present environment – between creation and consummation lies conservation – but it does deliver us from hoping only in the present world. There is something much better. A day will dawn when the Master himself will return, destroy evil and create all things new. A sinless world will be an environmentally safe world.

****

LESSON 8

The Environment

True or False

1. T F 'Green issues' aren't really very important.
2. T F Conservation is a Christian concern.
3. T F The world came into existence through evolution.
4. T F God made a brilliant world which he now lets run by cause-and-effect laws.
5. T F We are stewards of God's world and should run it according to his will.
6. T F Lack of thanksgiving is a cause of God's anger.
7. T F It doesn't matter how you treat animals.
8. T F God wants everything to have times of rest.
9. T F Greed is the cause of most of our environmental problems.

10. T F The environment will go on getting better and better indefinitely.

Group Discussion

1. Discuss how the Sabbath principle needs applying in our modern society.
2. Consider practical conservation steps you could encourage and initiate in your community.
3. Discuss the impact of the West's industrial requirements on the Third World.

Personal Assignment

1. Check out the 'environmental friendliness' of your own lifestyle. Do you need to make some changes?
2. Write down six aspects of the gospel that have a direct bearing on how we treat our environment – for example, repenting of greed.
3. Pray for justice for the victims of industrial pollution.

True or False

1.F 2.T 3.F 4.F 5.T 6.T 7.F 8.T 9.T 10.F